THE FLUT

By the same author

THE HILL OF KRONOS
THE LIGHT GARDEN OF THE ANGEL KING

THE FLUTES OF AUTUMN

Peter Levi

HARVILL PRESS
8 Grafton Street, London W1
1983

Harvill Press Ltd
is distributed by
William Collins Sons & Co. Ltd
London · Glasgow · Sydney · Auckland
Toronto · Johannesburg

The publishers would like to thank the estate of Carola Oman for permission to quote from *Memories of an Oxford Childhood*, published by Hodder & Stoughton Ltd (p. 81); Faber & Faber Ltd for permission to quote from 'Under Which Lyre' from *Collected Works of W. H. Auden* (p. 129); and Oxford University Press for permission to quote from 'Briggflatts' from *Basil Bunting's Collected Poems* (p. 179).

British Library Cataloguing in Publication Data
Levi, Peter
The flutes of autumn.
1. Levi, Peter 2. Authors, English – 20th century
– Biography
I. Title
821'.912 PR6023.E912Z/

ISBN 0-00-216246-6

First published 1983

Photoset in Sabon by Rowland Phototypesetting Ltd
Bury St Edmunds, Suffolk
Printed and bound by
Robert Hartnoll Ltd, Bodmin

For Deirdre

CONTENTS

The Flutes of Autumn

Und leise tönen im Rohr die dunkeln Flöten
des Herbstes . . .

And in the reeds the dark flutes of autumn
mutter their undertone . . .

G. Trakl, *Grodek* (1914)

CHAPTER ONE

Suburban Shades

> Our proud suburban shades
> Of branching elm, that never sun pervades.
>
> Cowper's translation of
> Milton's Latin elegy

I WAS BORN IN a crowded suburban house at Ruislip, with a long garden full of elm trees and apple trees and the comforting rattle of trains. Our road was asphalted, but half the village roads were still gravel; they had ruts that Mr Collins said you could have drowned a horse in. Vast green elm trees were everywhere in the gardens of those houses, along the lines of the old hedges. Only a few cottages and a pub near our house were more than fifty years old, but to me it all looked everlasting. The mint under the James Grieve apple tree had obviously been there for ever. So had the Japanese cherries and the flowering almonds and the damson trees in front gardens. The milkman still had a horse, so did old Mr Collins with the dung cart. My brother's godmother, who was a French lady from Selfridge's hats department, used to run out with a shovel to pick up horse manure for her garden. Motor cars were unusual, and my father drove down the middle of the road, hooting a tune as he came home. In the afternoons in summer, a man came round with an ice-cream cart on a tricycle, ringing his bell. He sold triangular sticks of water ice. You could pick twenty or thirty different kinds of leaves out of the hedges between our wooden gate and my first school.

Does it sound idyllic? All the same it was more and more

suburban every year. The Uxbridge-line station was a short walk away, and we went to pantomimes in Harrow and in London and had our shoes bought at Daniel Neal's. The best local walk was the golf course path, a green lane between hedges that led out into the fields towards Harefield and the real country; but the hazards of that path were mud and riding school horses and flying golf-balls.

Before the war, Ruislip was still an outer suburb, it was a village really; that scruffy umbracious margin where the town was just beginning to dissolve the countryside in its dark acid. But you could still walk across the fields then as far as Harrow and never meet anything but cows. Harrow gasometer was visible from our road. It glinted in the sunlight, and it seemed to me as romantic in the distance as a Norman castle. On dark, rainy evenings the gaslights in our road had beams like the jaws of crocodiles. There was one just under the almond tree outside the nursery window.

Our neighbours were extremely mixed. I can recall a man with one wooden leg who worked in the Mint, a women's hat designer, a family of gypsies, a German Jewish refugee dentist in a very modern house, a jewel thief the police got, and a soldier who won a VC and became a general later. Beyond our back hedge lived an extremely minor poet who worked in the city, a parody of Roy Fuller without the talent. Down the road lived another family, considered a bit strange, who put on Greek plays in their garden and went in for extraordinary dances. I think they must have belonged to London University. One year my father and his friends got extremely drunk at the golf club dance, but most entertainment was in London and most jobs were there. You spoke of going 'down the village', though it was a very small hill, but always 'up to London': town meant the West End and the city was the City. One of the first times I can remember satisfying a secret topographic curiosity was when I discovered on foot, on my own, how the City was joined on to places like Baker Street Station. But that was later, and it was not until I was grown up that I had finally traced the course of the Thames all the way from Windsor to the Tower.

We are going too fast. It is hard to give a true impression of a private world so limited as mine was. Because my father was quite well off then, and a Jewish businessman who had made his friends long ago, we knew rather few people in Ruislip; but because he was also a Catholic, we had very few Jewish friends, and saw only a few of his vast family. Having been a private soldier in the 1914 war, he had a certain contempt for officers and their social class. We grew up in a world of our own, as he had done. Because we used the Underground and taxis, London to me was like a vast rabbit-warren; I knew none of the connections above ground between the rabbit-holes. The port of London was a place of thrilling romance, seldom visited, where my father's carpets arrived. His business letter heading carried a wonderful rigmarole of which I was very proud, with the names of his brothers, and the magic closing words 'And At Constantinople'. But to this day I have never seen the Thames below Greenwich or maybe Dagenham.

When I ask myself what I thought England was like at that time, since I had little concept of the British Isles, the answer must come from holidays, and from the Rigg sisters. The Christmas before my parents married, my mother's father discovered by chance that my father's man-servant was cheating him most outrageously over the Christmas accounts, so, to my father's long-lasting regret and lamentation, the man was got rid of. The servant who saw my mother through the first mysteries of ladies' afternoon bridge parties, and whether to wear a hat at lunch, was a formidable housekeeper called Mrs Andrews. I notice women's hats have already turned up three times in these few pages; that must say something about the outer suburbs in the 1930s. Mrs Andrews had to go in her turn, because of a conniving relationship with the butcher. After that we went to the new Sainsbury, which I think was then called the Pay and Take. It had a huge St Bernard dog half asleep outside it. And the Rigg family arrived, one by one.

They came from Whitley Bay, near Blyth, at a time when jobs were hard to find. They were so poor that although they lived on the beach, just opposite the most wonderful sands in England, the two older sisters never learned to swim because they never had swimming costumes. In the early thirties, Cissy, the second sister, was already working in Ruislip for a fearsome lady who locked up the tea and the biscuits. It was Cissy who spotted my mother's advertisement and brought the eldest sister, Agnes, down from Blyth to take it up. Soon afterwards, as there was enough work in our house for two, Cissy joined Agnes; then, so as not to break up the family, the youngest one, Elsie, came as well. Elsie was only a girl really, so she got most of the pleasanter jobs. We loved them all, and they loved us, but I think my mother loved Cissy most. Feeling the loneliness, their mother and father came for prolonged visits which I think we all hoped might last a lifetime. I have no idea how everyone fitted into our house. Mrs Rigg was a tiny lady, admittedly. She used to shelter under the kitchen table from thunderstorms. Alone? Mr Rigg was a retired ship's painter in bad health from industrial disease. I hardly recollect him, but before we ever met he was the most romantic person in my life. He had painted the *Warspite* and the *Hood*. To look at, he was a little like Andy Capp.

To us they were almost foreigners, not because of class, of which I was unconscious until I had it hammered into me at school, and certainly not because of the accent – I loved accents of every kind and picked them up like measles: it was just the vast distance of the North. The whole of England outside London seemed to be country, and the North being further away was an extreme case of country. Towns were smaller cases of London or bigger cases of Ruislip: on the whole they were like Harrow. The life of the North was deeply stirring, coal was dug and the great ships were built there; the people were heavenly and warm and funny, like the Riggs. The coal miners, the true salt of the earth, lived in tiny houses, very snug like Mr Lambert the milkman's house; they had baths in zinc tubs in the kitchen, far more exciting than the bathroom or the nursery, but they never let anyone wash their backs for fear of losing their strength, except once a year. They had a collie-dog or a greyhound. The coal mines were in the middle of the country. The miners were very loyal. In the summer they went to Blackpool, and I had a postcard of Blackpool Illuminations, which I thought must be the most beautiful thing in the world. Cissy was going to take me there one day. I never did get to see them though, except once in the far distance on a summer night, from the top of the Lancashire Fells. The war came and altered everything.

We went on holidays to the Isle of Wight and the coast of North Wales, which I hardly remember, then once to a house at Rustington, where we played cricket in the garden for hours as long and happy as whole years, and where my father broke his kneecap, and once to Kingsbridge in Devon. I fell in love with the sea, and screamed with pleasure when I saw it from a train. The extent of England began to dawn on me, the impressive, mountainous height of cliffs and rocks, the size and power of waves like rampaging houses, the glittering sea with its ten thousand moods. I was ripe for Shakespeare really, and by a freak of good luck I discovered him when I was six, through mooning over the namby-pamby stories in Lamb's *Tales*, and demanding the real thing. There were not a lot of books in our house, except children's books. The Lamb's *Tales from Shakespeare* was an illustrated prize book won by one of my three uncles who died in 1916. Everyone we knew in childhood had dead fathers or cousins or uncles from that war. Everyone still called it the Great War, or just the War. The idea of it utterly dominated our secret thoughts as nothing else ever has done.

The older men who were alive then had often fought in earlier wars. An old man who I think was a gardener showed me his medals, which were his greatest treasure. They were big, gleaming silver things, with campaign bars for battles in Africa against the Zulus, and in India against the Afghans. If I remember this rightly, he said he had fought at Maiwand, which I read the other day was the last time in history that a young officer, who used to be called Ensign, carried the regimental colours into battle. That officer was always shot of course, and after Maiwand the rank and tradition were abolished. To my old gardener, all battles were much the same, all enemies were fuzzy-wuzzies. If I calculate his age rightly, he was too old for 1914; he was about eighty in 1936. My father was a good and generous man, and perhaps had done him some service. Today I feel as if I imagined it all. Yet I remember him, and I remember his medals, and his story conveys just the quality of my childish thoughts, as I played with toy soldiers on the nursery floor. No one talked about the details of the Great War to children. We found it all out slowly, as we grew up.

War did affect the extent of the world in our imaginations. In the country until recently it was quite common to meet simple working people who had hardly left their village except for years and years of imperial campaigning as young men. I knew an old hedger and ditcher in Oxfordshire who had been in India for fifteen years, and an old railway worker on the obscurest of branch lines, a paradise of badgers and overgrown embankments, who had a bullet-wound in the backside which he got while he was having a drink behind a rock on Christmas Day in the Khyber Pass. An old man in the Fox in Chipping Norton told me one winter's morning about the Battle of the Somme. It was beautiful he said, miles and miles of guns and carriages perfectly in line, all the brasses shining, all the horses perfectly groomed, like the Oxfordshire Show. And then it started.

Places even in England were more completely different then than they are now. If I never had any doubts that England was one place, that was because of the Great War, and the sea, and the Rigg family, and then Shakespeare I suppose. Of course Shakespeare never knew the whole of England. His North was as misty as mine. Only the other day I found him making a Duke of Northumberland amazed at the vast, wild Cotswolds, 'these high, wild hills and rough, uneven ways'. He can never have seen Stainmore or the upper Tyne. Gilbert White in the 1780s was still speaking about the Sussex Downs as mountains. It was the railways really that revealed England. In the 1760s you sailed from Glasgow to London, and it might take you a month. In the 1930s, on empty roads in a big Buick, it used to take my father a day or two. Yet I still thought Scotland was as separate as any Scottish Nationalist could wish. What I thought of as wild country was the Isle of Wight, and then Devonshire.

At Kingsbridge, we lived on a farm. I saw animals slaughtered, and learnt from the farmer's daughter to steal apples and hide in a hayloft. We swam in a cove, with a boy of thirteen who was her younger brother; he could swim like an otter and dive from the rocks. I wanted passionately to be like him, but thirteen was a long way off. I think it was on that holiday that I fell genuinely in love with the country itself, and the smell of leaves and cows. I remember that once it rained on and off all day, and in some light, gleaming shower in the late afternoon I went for a walk by myself. Maybe it was the first time I ever did that. The smell of hedges was intoxicating and the intricacy of what grew in them was enthralling, not so much a tangle, which it was, as a density. Compared to anything I knew, that rank hedge parsley and the shooting, flowering weeds, even the thistles in the fields, all seemed a wild and intimate world. Since that time I have seen so many vast dawns as cold and salty as the sea, so many suns sinking into the mouldy west, so many starry or misty nights, that the small scale of those first hedges and bird-twitters might seem precious and far away. But that smell and the wet feel of the grass and the weeds really were like falling in love; they drew from me the most passion I was capable of. It was the diversity of the world, not its antiquity, that was so exciting. Later we come to know it as antiquity, something that survived, and then as something lost. Lost by our own death, if in no other way.

Then came the war. In that same summer of 1939 we went

to stand in the grass ditch by the wire fence to watch the first squadron of Hurricanes ever built arrive at Northolt aerodrome. They were the fastest thing we had ever seen. Indeed they were the fastest thing almost anyone had ever seen at that time. They were round one of the Battle of Britain, and being a Jewish family we already knew it. They came low down over our heads, whizzing out of the sky. My father joined the Civil Defence, flopped about in cowpats, and learnt to deliver babies on buses. My mother learnt to drive an ambulance and wear trousers. She must have just acquired her first car, which greatly extended our range in Ruislip. We used to go to the common, a windy brow of hill with gorse bushes, and into Ruislip Woods and Mad Bess Woods for picnics and games, stalking one another through the bracken. There used to be fritillaries in a field up there; now not even the field exists any more.

Ruislip before the war was not by any means as John Betjeman imagined it. Nor for that matter was Slough. Pinner had a church dedicated to a saint called Philomena who did miracles. She held the unusual distinction of never having really been alive at all; she was a popular fiction of the last century. Ruislip shared with Pinner a minute stream called the Pin. It was little more than a wet ditch with sticklebacks in it. Did it flow somewhere into the Thames? Or was it a tributary of Ruislip Reservoir, a murky green lake full of weeds that belonged to the Grand Union Canal? The chief pleasure of Pinner was Cuckoo Hill, a headlong cycle ride between very green hedges. In 1939 we were just about to move to a bigger house in another village, but we never did move, and the other house was requisitioned for the Air Force in the first month of the war. In the next year or two, Ruislip suddenly begot five or six factories and huge housing estates. The aerodrome sprouted a whole village of its own, full of Polish babies. Ruislip was drowned in those vast tidal flats of the London suburbs that stretch now for twenty miles.

I am not sure when I first thought about the history of

Ruislip. As a place to live in we liked it, I even loved it, but we always spoke of it with affectionate contempt, almost as if we came from somewhere better and might go back there: as if we were Londoners. I know I envied cockneys; I tried hard to hear Bow Bells from Ruislip. I think my usual accent was a bit cockney. But the only taproot I really had was a withered one, feeling out through my father's warehouse in Houndsditch with its smell of hessian and rolled carpets, towards an infinitely distant Constantinople. The fact of my mother being born in Harrow, my father probably in Croydon or in Hackney, and my mother's two surviving brothers living in Wimbledon and Colchester gave me no romantic feeling about those places, only an appalled curiosity. But Houndsditch and Billingsgate and the Tower of London seemed to me as distant and romantic as the sea, and as seldom visited. Certainly Ruislip during the war, much as I secretly loved it, was no fit object for any romantic meditations. I discovered that finally at fifteen, when I tried to write poems about it, in which the hills towards Denham had to stand for Kipling's or Belloc's Sussex Downs, and the straggling lines of elm trees towards Harefield did their best to sum up all Rupert Brooke's nostalgic feelings.

The war brought us children at least one benefit. Because travelling was difficult, we did at least get to know our immediate district very well. That was the last moment when it was possible to get the sense of a whole life that was dying and a whole countryside that was being devoured. Things speak the truth on their deathbed. But it was our luck that work in the fields was still or once again done by hand. You saw geese and ducks on village greens, and more horses were brought back to work in the war than would ever be seen again. Farm carts a hundred or two years old were still in common use. The landlord of the Six Bells still remembered delivering his hay into London and coming home drunk in the haycart with the reins left to a mare that knew her own way home. Old men were still alive further afield than Ruislip who had been used to mowing their way to London every year in the hay season.

They hired themselves out to farm after farm until they got there. Even the London social season before the war was tied to agriculture: I once heard an old flowerseller explain that it ended when the earliest lavender was cried in the streets. It was during the war that we learnt to ride horses, and I associate that, far more than school terms with their foul smells and rough games, with getting some sense of the seasons of the year, and some sense of the weather. We rode in all weathers.

We used to ride out to Ladygate Lane past an isolated pub called the Breakspear Arms, which we believed was named after the family of the first English Pope, to gallop in a field called Forty Acre. I am sure I had always known Ladygate Lane. It was an ordinary country road with mothy hedges, a sort of tan-coloured gravelly tarmac where a horse might get a pebble in its hoof or a children's pony might grab a mouthful of leaves. If you went further you passed a watersplash where an overflowing stream ran across the road. When at last I got excited by the history of Ruislip, about the summer of 1941, I found that Ladygate Lane was all that was left of an old monastery, and Sharp's Lane, another gravelly place with no pavements, but inside the village, was all that was left of an old retired highwayman called Sharp. It will be seen that Ruislip had no history in any serious sense. History had happened mostly at places like the Tower of London, and I thought it began with the Romans. All that Ruislip could boast was its obscure Anglo-Saxon name, its buried agricultural prosperity, its parish church and its manor farm buildings, an enormous empty barn and a working forge. And the woods of course.

All the same Ruislip began to work on me. Long before I ever lived in the real country, and long before I understood even the word archaeology, I had begun to see that all places buried and embodied their own histories, and that what was left, what you loved and maybe used every day, somehow included, or somehow was that history. History made everywhere romantic. The past was the bones of the landscape. Loving any history was loving a place that embodied it, and hating that place to change. If you loved a place, you automatically found out its history: the Romans or whatever it might be. There was nothing unusual in what I felt. I remember a friend of mine at perhaps eleven being told that a particular tower was eleventh century and the oldest piece of stone building in Oxford. He stroked it and stroked it, very gently, and hated to leave it. About the age of rocks or fossils I knew nothing, and nor did he. Prehistory was a blank. Geology was one of my most impassioned boyhood crazes, but that was because I loved stones. I never cared as much as I should about their age or their formation. Nor did any of us care then about social or local history as people study it today. That still seems to me a rather middle class kind of subject. But I wish I had known then that Forty Acre records a standard measure of the eighteenth century enclosure acts. What comes first is a passion for the places themselves, for the body and bones of England and of all Britain. Or that was what came first to me. The longing curiosity to read the landscape like reading a book is only one of its expressions.

What I could read of Ruislip was simple enough. The road we lived in was called King's End. Properly it was King's End Road. I found out its origin from an old map in a pamphlet I bought; where five roads met at the top of King's End, a few houses away from us, there used to be something called Little King's End Green. The houses at the crossroads formed a kind of semicircle. Where Great King's End Green was I never discovered, and perhaps I had the whole question upside down, but this was how I figured it out. When the monastery was suppressed, which was Benedictine and belonged to Bec in Normandy, the land went to King's College Cambridge. The little sprinkling of older cottages behind the White Bear pub must have once been a kind of hamlet attached to Ruislip. The roads that met there told their own story: they were King's End, Ickenham Road, which came up from old Ruislip and the parish church and went away past the White Bear towards Ickenham, Sharp's Lane, and a quiet lane with hedges and few houses called Wood Lane. That had a steeper hill than King's End, and led nowhere much except to some stables; it only got asphalted in my memory. It trickled vaguely away towards Field End Farm where Ruislip still ended in 1939, in the London direction. In Wood Lane we tried to teach my mother to ride a bicycle during the war, with small success I am afraid, because she always got frightened and steered into sanctuary in the hedge.

Ickenham was the next village. In those days Ickenham duckpond was full of ducks and dark green and very muddy. My brother once fell into it. Beyond Ickenham lay Hillingdon, a small, new-seeming place on the Western Avenue. We seldom or never went beyond that huge highway except in summer, toiling uphill on bicycles morning after morning up Swakelys Avenue, past a place called Gospel Oak and a lane that led to Harefield, then over the roundabout where the Western Avenue still ended until about 1945, and across a heath with a strange water-tower, to Uxbridge swimming baths. They were a world of pure, almost surrealist modernity: enormous open-air baths of light blue water, with dashing modernistic concrete buildings, a three-storey café with a sunbathing roof, and a diving-board like a sky-diving tower. Before the war, Elsie used to take us there, by bus I suppose. As I write I can remember the prickly feeling of wet woollen swimming-trunks, and our faded pink and white swimming towels worn smooth from over-use. Uxbridge baths were unashamedly, thrillingly modern. I am not sure if I could get anyone else to admire their architecture today as much as I did then, and yet I believe that nothing else in that world would so immediately have convinced an ancient Greek that England was civilized.

Suburban children swim at the baths. Pools and rivers come a little later. Shakespeare's Avon and his Thames with the wanton boys that swim on bladders were as remote from my childhood as Chaucer's world. But one must remember that down to the 1950s, in remote villages without any kindly river, no one could swim at all. Uxbridge itself meant nothing to me. It was a busy place with a few bony, elegant houses, the end of the London Underground and the first big bus station I ever knew. It never occurred to me then to wonder what oxen had crossed the bridge at Uxbridge, or who the Icca or the Ick was who founded Ickenham, or even what Ruislip was like before the Normans took it over. Even of the Normans I knew only the name of someone called Arnulph de Hesdin, who left a little green bump like a Christmas pudding surrounded by a scummy pond, once his castle and his moat, down by the public library. It never occurred to me to ask about the old approach to London from the west, before the Western Avenue was built.

Yet the Western Avenue was obviously new; it went by us a mile or two our side of Uxbridge; the Bath Road passed right through the town. To put it another way, not only the Bath Road goes through Uxbridge, and runs on south of the Berkshire Downs towards the south-west, but also the Oxford road which runs on through High Wycombe. The Western Avenue is a short cut to that road. I knew about Roman soldiers' roads like the Fosse Way and the Icknield Way and Akeman Street, but nothing at all about the droving tracks, some of which are more ancient still. In fact the route for Welsh cattle to the London market used to pass by Uxbridge to Harrow-on-the-Hill. Where the Western Avenue runs past Northolt was heathland in my childhood. Gypsy ponies grazed there: at one time the big skewbald drum horses of the Household Cavalry used to be bred in those unkempt fields. The availability of land to make the great airports says a good deal about the amount of heath there must once have been around London. That is the way the cattle must have moved.

We were certainly conscious as children of the wild raggedness of those places. One of my favourite spots for riding, which all had to be within an hour of the stables, was called Eastcote Grub Grounds. That was where I rode Blaze, a young half-trained racehorse with the softest of soft noses. It was a good place to gallop, being unfrequented common land of no obvious beauty, with whole plantations of wild bushes and young trees dotted about. I can still remember the coldness of the rain there, the mists of midwinter and the tattered coming of the spring. Eastcote Grub Grounds had that invigorating untamed quality mingled with melancholy that specially belongs to the waste ground outside great cities and which is like a smell of home to me. Gypsies were often camping, and the horses shied at the bright rags and tatters of cloth they left in the branches. Being between London and the real country, the region around Ruislip was thickly populated with gypsies.

They came to the doors of houses selling clothes pegs; they did no great harm, though their encampments were unenviably sordid and they looked cold and hungry. My father once brought home a lost child some gypsies had abandoned on Christmas Day. Many years later, in a Manchester hostel for drunken vagrants, I met that child's father. He was Irish, and he told me a weird tale about the curse of vagrancy put on tinkers, because they passed by the cross of Christ, and all other men refused to make the nails. It was a drunken babble, but the belief that metal-workers are under a curse and outside human societies is very old indeed.

The only intimate, familiar connection I had with Anglo-Saxon England was one of my names. Peter Chad Tigar Levi was as odd a collection of names as one might wish for, and a great embarrassment at school. My mother's family was called Tigar, supposedly after a shipwrecked Spaniard from the Armada who knew no other word intelligible to the English but the name of the ship's dog. That happened in Cornwall. As for believing it, I can only claim that I went so far as to check the date of the spelling, and I found Tigar in the sixteenth century in the Clef des Champs. My mother had an ancient clerical uncle, a friar who lived in Leicester on a miserable diet imposed by doctors, which he never broke except to eat curry with my father. They had both ruined their digestions in the tropics. This great-uncle of mine was crazy about English saints. It was all part of the Catholic claim to be the proper English church and not a nineteenth century Italian mission, I imagine, but it made me learn a name I venerate. As a tiny child I was called Chad or Peter Chad, Peter being at first a mere concession to normality, but apparently I protested early, and I now have no memory of ever being addressed as Chad.

Saint Chad had a brother called Chedd. They were trained at Lindisfarne in the seventh century by Aidan, the founder, and something from that wild place with its fawning seals and its mewing gulls and its North Sea wind remained with him. Aidan being an Irishman, Chad was partly schooled in Ireland, without doubt severely. Oswiu, the King of Northumberland, being vexed by the long absence of Saint Wilfrid of York, chose Chad to take Wilfrid's place, and Chad took the fatal step of having himself consecrated bishop by some southern bishops not well thought of by Canterbury. Wilfrid came home in the end and sulked at Ripon for several years, until Canterbury restored him to York. Chad retired quite happily to a monastery on the edge of the North Yorkshire moors, but they dug him out of it again, and made him the first bishop of the Mercians. This was his dear wish and the greatest opportunity of his life. The Mercians were a ferocious and a pagan people. I suppose we must owe Christianity in a large part of Europe to the urge in Christian monks like Chad to Christianize their persecutors. Lindisfarne lies in the shelter of Bamburgh Head, and Aidan in his hermitage on the Inner Farne rock saw Penda, King of the Mercians, burning down Bamburgh Castle.

Here we touch on one of the principal themes of this book, but of course as a child I misunderstood anything I knew about the Dark Ages; they must wait. Chad was consecrated as a missionary bishop to one of the most interesting tribes in Europe. He travelled, as I used to believe, on foot, but when he was eighty years old the Archbishop of Canterbury insisted on giving him a donkey. The English Midlands were not at all civilized in the seventh century, and Mercia was a vast territory. Chad died at Lichfield, in a monastery which he founded near where the Cathedral now is. His dead body was kept in a wooden box shaped like a little house, with a hole in one side so that people could put their hands in for a pinch of dust. I had only the vaguest idea as a child how far Mercia extended, or even where Lichfield was, but I would have liked the box. At school we were supposed to back the Anglo-Saxons of Wessex against the rest. History as we learnt it had a Churchillian ring. I think I imagined Alfred had civilized England, although the pictures we had of him made him as improbable as the little fair-haired Child Jesus with the wooden porringer. I hated porridge. Still, I did feel strongly about Saint Chad. I was glad to find out later about Dr Johnson's indignation over the melting down of the lead from Lichfield Cathedral roof: 'What they shall melt, it were just that they should swallow.'

Having the secret name of Chad was my connection with the North, where the friendly Rigg sisters came from, and the Midlands, which I hardly distinguished. The Midlands are in fact rather hard to distinguish, because Birmingham squats in the middle of them like an obese spider with tentacles twenty miles long. That was not how I thought of Birmingham as a boy. It was thrilling to me. It seemed freer and more modern than Ruislip, more in the atmosphere of Uxbridge swimming baths and the architecture of hope. I stayed there in the war for a fortnight with a friend from school. His father was a possible Liberal candidate for Parliament who never actually stood; he was a dentist in Selly Oak. The most beautiful and peaceful parts of Birmingham we hardly saw at that time, though I did see them by good fortune in the sixties, just a few years before Birmingham was devastated by a more crushing wave of modernity than the 1930s had ever known. We used to bicycle out from Selly Oak ten or twenty miles to a farm, to help bring in the hay. My friend's mother taught me an Aston Villa football song, 'You can't stop Broome from scoring.' I began to see the truth of the great British axiom that the further north you go the nicer the people get. Birmingham is halfway to Newcastle.

I went on another wartime journey to Northwich in Cheshire, but I had so little notion of regional geography that it could as easily have been Norfolk or Monmouthshire. It was a long, hot journey in a very slow train to Crewe. Beyond Ruislip golf course, which the train crossed, I am still unclear which way it went. Journeys like that had many pauses between embankments tangled in strange flowers that seemed to grow nowhere else. The rosebay willowherb, which we called fireweed, was just beginning to be one of them. They say it came from Canada in cargoes of timber, but it must be volcano-bred, because it likes cinders, and spread all over England by railway lines to flourish in the ruins of London after the Blitz. You see willowherb everywhere today, but it always reminds me of the bombed buildings round Saint Paul's. Better the ruins and the rosebay willowherb perhaps, than the peering towers that surround Saint Paul's now.

At Northwich my friend's mother lived in a country pub, which she ran while her husband the landlord was away. I remember a forest, and riding in the forest on a strong little pony. The pub was named after a greyhound whose monument stood opposite. He ran the Derby course against a famous racehorse and won, but he went blind doing it. Or did the racehorse go blind and the hound die of heart failure like the runner from Marathon? It was an affecting story that everyone was proud of knowing, myself included. The place was very quiet in wartime, and the pub tranquil and pastoral by modern standards. No one had petrol, which may be why I recollect from that summer only flat fields and grazing cattle and glinting canals.

The war was more serious than I make it sound, even for children. That boy's father was a motorcyclist who used to be dropped in France before D-day to spy out the roads. Later on he was at the head of the first column to reach Dachau, and the photographs he sent home to his son were the first I understood of what Dachau contained. They were the worse for being simple little snapshots. My friend passed them to me secretly, under a desk, as if they were things no one ought to see, things that never should have seen the sun. And some boys' fathers were killed. Mine nearly was, more than once, just by bombs. My mother took me to visit a woman in King's End (why me? why take a child? was what I thought) who had just lost the fourth of her four sons. We had air-raid shelters built onto our house; by now my father was an air-raid warden, but just once or twice he brought me outside at night, to see the aeroplanes fighting among the stars and searchlights. The morning after the Germans hit London docks, the whole of the early morning sky was full of an infinite red dawn in the wrong direction.

The *Hood* went down with nearly all her crew in terribly cold water. *Warspite* went down. The Rigg family separated soon after the beginning of the war. They were still with us for the first air raid, because that happened during a picnic in Mad Bess Woods; nothing passed overhead but one tiny aeroplane, innocently straying. Elsie had gone home from the woods to fetch something; she was just passing the police station by the alms houses in the bottom of the village when the wail of the siren started up. Old Mrs Rigg was still in Ruislip then. She was terrified of bombs, which she rightly thought of as a more undiscriminating form of thunderstorm, so she and Mr Rigg went home to Blyth, and beloved Cissy went with her to look after them both. Cissy never married. She worked all her life on the Newcastle buses, looking after her parents and helping to keep them. Years later when my mother was dying she came back and looked after her too. Young Elsie went away to the war in uniform. She did marry, and named her daughter Gillian after my sister; years afterwards my sister was headmistress of that Gillian's school. And Agnes, adorable, cross Agnes who stood so much teasing and returned it, and hid so much love and showed it, Agnes for whom I proudly paraded my first wicked words, stayed on with us cooking her way through the Blitz, until she married Jimmy Collins, driver of the council dust lorry, son of old Mr Collins with the cartloads of dung, whose farm under Ruislip Woods was the last one left in the village.

Sometimes in the evening our house was full of airmen my father brought home from the pub, though much more often he had just a few cronies who are no part of this story. The places the airmen came from were completely remote. If not Polish, they were Canadian or South African. I think I supposed that somewhere else there must be a purely English Air Force. The war news was full of half visualized words like Marshalling Yard, and the names of foreign places, the Ruhr, Omsk, Tomsk, Tobruk. One had a sense of enormous extent and endless confusion. The maps of Europe were not only most difficult to interpret, they were all out of date now. Reality was the sketch-maps in the newspapers, with a front, and a shaded area for the enemy, and enormous black arrows for each intended advance. Inside England, one got to know of places by their being bombed. It was like a huge darkness illuminated only by the fires of air raids.

Our own raiding aeroplanes as the war went on swarmed across the sky in such numbers that you felt you could hear the sky shake. We sucked our barley-sugar. The dog whined. I still read England mostly in terms of a few plays by Shakespeare, and perhaps for that reason I noticed as a child something profoundly and solemnly Shakespearean about the war in the air. I had no great illusions about Dunkirk. The brother of a friend of mine at school was bayoneted there, and my own half-brother caught pneumonia so badly that he got invalided out of the army. They made him an officer in the Catering Corps and rather curiously sent him to Iceland. My mother explained to me how Dunkirk was a great victory really, because of the little ships sailing to the rescue, including some belonging to my Uncle Ned. But I was only just nine and asked some naïve questions. A moral victory, my mother insisted. I asked what that meant. Then my father took me aside and told me it was a terrible defeat, but not to let my mother know. I believe it was then I realized how we were going to win the war.

We were brought up, at God knows what cost to heart and nerve, to be quite fearless of air raids and perfectly certain that we should win in the end. Bets were made at supper on nights of what was called a bomber's moon about whether or what time the Germans would come over. We collected spent bullets, pieces of shell and bomb, fragments of exploded aeroplane. My father had a certain humorous contempt for danger, and a self-mockery. He set up his Air-Raid Warden post in a brick shed specially built in the car park of his usual pub. He payed for half a Spitfire in a City subscription as one might buy half a cold roast chicken. An old-fashioned cast-iron gallantry extended to the bottom of his soul. It had a London Jewish flavour I associate nowadays with certain elderly taxi drivers. The manual labours of the war, the lifting and carrying, and maybe the worries as well, gave him heart attacks. On his sixtieth birthday he drank a lot at lunch, and then made a speech about his two young sons away at the war, serving their country, unable to be present. I think we were eleven and thirteen. He was a loyal reader of the *Express*.

My mother's views of gallantry were exaggerated. It is not quite fair to say they were based on what she called the flower of England, who died in the Great War; like everybody's views even in childhood, they were a special reading of her own experience of life. Her father was a stockbroker caught out with continental stocks and shares in August 1914. He was hammered on the Stock Exchange in the week war broke out. He never worked full time again, or at anything but financial journalism. He had five sons and a younger daughter. Two were shot dead in France within a fortnight of their commissions, and the third, who was still at school, heard the news from a boy delivering the fatal telegram. He was not a hundred yards from home, but he seems to have had a heart attack on the way, and it killed him. The fourth survived; Fred was sweet-natured, wooden and uncle-like; he married his dead brother's fiancée as the custom was, though I doubt if he was ever precisely in love. The youngest brother was sent as a conscript when the war was over to fight in Russia against the wicked Communists. He suffered nightmare experiences then, and he lived an unhappy life afterwards.

My mother was ten in 1914; her childhood cannot have been all cream and roses. In her happiest stories about it she was eight or nine. The Catholic religion as she understood it added to her father's ruin and the death of her brothers an intensely romantic and isolating factor. She was an intelligent woman, but the 1939 war, which ended with her forty-first year, broke her nerve, and she arrived in the end near to collapse on the threshold of old age, finding the need to use her intelligence for the first time. She had never read a serious book or understood a newspaper not pre-digested until she took to reading Trollope and *The Times* on her deathbed. But her favourite brother, the one who read the telegram, had done very well at school; they said he showed promise as a writer. The *Lamb's Tales* was his. So although she left school herself at the earliest possible age, she was most eager that we should read and be educated. At the same time her moral views were uncompromising. The dead in battle were like Catholic martyrs. They were like her brothers. Courage was so automatic one never questioned what it was. Nothing daunted her: nothing daunted my ideal self. Faith was absolute and tranquil. She breathed gallantry like a dragon breathing fire. She was quite impossible to argue with, as my father advised us often. With him she never argued.

If I have seemed to dwell too long on these family matters, that is because to describe my childhood, my simple opening of the eyes, I am forced to explain my generation, but in order to do that I must explain myself and my family. In wartime England one was conscious not only of the war, but of everything, even the way one felt about snow or the moon or hanging woods turning colour on the brow of a hill, or the fruit in the garden, or the name Yorkshire or Gloucestershire (which battalion?), was affected by war. During the war and for years afterwards I saw every landscape as a battlefield; I heard the sullen, melancholy crump of bombs and the night noises of air battles inside my head whenever I was anxious or in trouble until I was past thirty. At the age of eleven I was a one man Dad's Army. I know of another boy of the same generation who spent hours and hours in later life riding his farm tractor and working in the fields, always thinking and thinking of different ways of escaping from Colditz. My own obsession was a cross between the Home Guard and the European resistance: along what ditch to creep, inside what woods to hide, by what hedgeside to disappear, to evaporate into the English landscape.

The sinister side of all this was merely imaginative, I dare say self-induced, but partly no doubt determined by films. There was something more than slightly false in the heroic atmosphere of films in the 1940s. Cinemas were emotional brothels. We were drugged with war-dreams from which you came out dizzy into the light. Life itself offered greater and more interesting heroism, and it was the moments when those wartime films did just touch on what we recognized as real that filled me and my friends with such exultation as boys. For one thing, they showed a lot of landscape in them. Vicars cycled down country lanes. The heroes lived in lush countryside, or they listened to birds or walked on a cliff, and England itself, seen from the air, was the mightiest symbol of all. The scaly sea, the glimmering white cliffs, and the British fleet meant something in the forties even Shakespeare had never foreseen. When the heroes of those films thought about England, they thought about it as seen by a zooming camera, and as seen from the air. Was that really how I learnt to love the English landscape? I certainly identified with everything that was felt in those films.

Nowadays my loyalty is sad and dogged; it is an attachment (which will never be rooted out) to the English people as I have known them for two thirds of a lifetime, a vast extension of the

Rigg family. Of course that takes for granted some abstract words like liberty, but when I say England, what I think of instinctively is the place itself, its diversity and its beauty and its antiquity.

CHAPTER TWO

Old Manners

If they have not forgotten their old manners,
But I fear they have forgotten them.

Lament for Arthur O'Leary

ONE EVENING in the sixties I found myself in Dublin, after some kind of poets' sabbath that was part of the Dublin festival. It was late. Drinks in the early evening in a hotel bar had led to drinks in the interval in a dark and generous pub that looked as if it figured in James Joyce, and that led on to drinks afterwards in a house, with biscuits and cheese which I never discovered. The poets' sabbath was an evening of translation, but half of it turned out to be translation into Irish, which some of the audience had not foreseen. At the drinks in the house I was hard pressed, because knowing no one, and being ignorant of Ireland, I gave the immediate clear impression, by dress and English accent, of an upper-class clerical booby, an Aunt Sally sent from heaven. I was asked if I knew Charles Haughey.

'The man who fell off his horse,' I said. It was the only thing I knew about him. At that time it may have been his principal claim to fame. He was unconscious for so long that it got into the English papers. They hated Haughey in that house. 'If there's one thing we hate in Ireland,' said my chief taunter, 'it's a Horse Protestant. But if there's one thing worse than a Horse Protestant, it's a Horse Catholic.' There followed a heated argument about whether this expressive proverb derived from the Elizabethan penal laws against Catholics owning good horses, or some other corner of the class war, race war, or national struggle. We strayed back to Haughey. 'Sure he was only brought up by the Brothers like meself,' said my friend. 'Were you?' 'I was beat black and blue by them.' We became best friends from that moment, because so was I.

My mother was proud of the fact that of all the varieties of blood that ran in her veins and in mine, not a drop was Irish. In the Harrow of her childhood, Catholics were outsiders, but Irish Catholics were worse outsiders. The Irish Christian Brothers, properly called the Brothers of the Christian Schools, were founded in the nineteenth century to produce a Catholic middle class, which in some raw sense of the word would have to be educated. They spread like wildfire all over the British Empire, in which they performed a useful function, and I went to one of their schools in England. My parents knew nothing about Catholic or any other schools, and my brother and I never realized until years afterwards what an odd place that was. It was a failed attempt, in some ways almost successful, at an English minor public school.

It was a boarding school near Bath. We wore stiff collars and black suits on Sundays from which it was very hard to remove Tate and Lyle's Golden Syrup, and everyone passed their exams; all the same, the school was very, very Irish. It even kept Irish time instead of British Summer Time. We knew the Catechism by heart; we were bullied and we were beaten. To this day, if the most flourishing institution in the National University of Ireland is the rugby club, and if the arts societies there huddle together in upper-middle-class conspiracies in the Dublin equivalent of Hampstead, the reason is that most people were brought up by the Brothers. The history and the politics I was taught at school were so wickedly prejudiced and so crazy that I automatically ignored them. Many years would have to pass before I began to understand, I think it was at Oxford, that the English really had treated the Irish badly, and the terrible stories about the Black and Tans were true. Of course I always had Irish friends, but they laughed at the

Brothers as much as anyone. Never can such concentrated, embittered, incessant propaganda have been so counterproductive.

We were sent away early to boarding school because my brother had asthma and I cried until I was sent with him. I was six. We went to that particular school only because it was so beautiful. My father thought, rightly in my view, that Stonyhurst looked like a prison, and drove away without going in. Beaumont was ruled out because of some cousins who were said to have taken to drink there as schoolboys. But Prior Park was an eighteenth-century building of grey Palladian beauty, an advertisement for Bath stone gazing downhill over a landscaped valley between hanging woods, with a dark romantic lake and a classical bridge like the one at Wilton, an austere grove of thin columns. Far away beyond that, like a backdrop, the stone city of Bath lay motionless with hills rising behind it. Hidden by slopes of grass between the house and the woods, Pope used to write his poems in a grotto furnished with ammonites. But the grotto was falling down, and I remember telling the Brothers that the ammonites were beginning to disappear. They did not mind much.

Whatever education I had in English landscape, in architecture, in corncrakes and nightjars and fields of cowslips and deep grass, in woods full of wild garlic, in the underworld of caves and abandoned quarries, in river swimming and in solitary reading and in wandering about at night, I got in that artificial paradise running gently to seed. I still recall the lustre of the buildings by moonlight as clearly as their splendid proportions in the sun. The school itself, as a school, was not gentle. I was two years young for my class, so for two or three years between eleven and fourteen, which felt like a century, I was monotonously, regularly bullied. I became hysterical, not very nice, and inwardly wild, untamable. Boarding school is so boring, and games with older boys were such purgatory, that nearly every day as I grew older I escaped into the woods or hid and read and read, or ran away to Bath to the junk shops and tea shops, the Dickensian back streets and the architecture.

The worst and the best thing about that schooling was that it was so completely philistine. The boys if they felt inclined were left quite alone to make their own discoveries, in art as in nature. No one told us what to like, only what to learn. The library, at least by modern standards, was good, just because it was so old-fashioned. Poetry was work, so you could get away with reading poetry during prep. As a little boy I read every narrative poem I could discover, and I still feel thankful to Sir Walter Scott for the comfort of those dark, rainy evenings. There I sat in the pit of what was called the Round Room, tousled and inky-fingered, the tiers of wooden benches round my head creaking and rustling with embryo doctors and baby bishops. My prep was finished and I was in romantic Scotland. The Brother in charge could not fault me for that. Even in class the poetry we were given was handed over unspoilt. You had to spell it, know what the words meant, and learn it by heart, and that was that. There are worse ways of teaching the *Ancient Mariner*. One boy before my time was famous for learning that whole poem by heart in one evening. He never went to a university or wrote anything; few Prior Park boys did. I think he was killed in the war. The only other way in which poetry was, I admit, rather magically touched, was in elocution lessons, where we learnt about the strange, wonderful noises it makes. We all had touches of provincial accent, so the elocution lessons were an important part of the enterprise.

But school and poetry are not my subject. I am not going to write about the sawing and carrying of logs, about crimes and punishments, about the pleasures of summer, the lilac tree, the unreformed dark kitchens and cellars and glory holes, or about chilblains. I could write many pages about the affliction of wartime chilblains and the horrors of feeling really cold and unloved. The worst moments were always in the Lent term, and I connect them with wet woollen gloves on a snowy slope, and later with playing hockey. Hockey was worse than rugby because of the freezing winds and showers of hailstones in which it was played. Also because you were hit more suddenly and harder, and the ball, the unwelcome centre of action, was harder to avoid. The plum-faced Irish Brother would scream at you, the other boys would yell derision. The Brothers boasted about an Irish form of hockey that was even worse, expressively called hurley. But then at last the whistle would blow; you could trail home more or less as slowly as you chose, shuffling through dead leaves for a mile along the road. You ducked through a wicket gate into the school grounds, wandered across the playing fields proper and downhill to the bootroom and the showers. The smell of unhappiness is the smell of the bootroom at Prior Park in the 1940s (unaltered for all I know since the 1840s).

The two things I studied most and understood least in the nine years I was imprisoned on that leafy and cloudy hillside were the Irish people and the English landscape. Today, the universe with all its stars is only as vast to me as this world was then. Ireland was as distant as America. Indeed I still feel more foreign in Dublin than I do in Boston or New York, which in a sense is the capital of mankind. The spelling *Telefon* in Gothic lettering on the phone boxes in Ireland is not quite a joke. Passing a golf course near Dublin gives me a cold shudder. The Brothers told stories about their own tough youth which included being beaten with the stick end of broken golf clubs, and the funny stories of the Dublin taxi drivers bring it all back like yesterday. What did I hate about the Brothers most? The scrubbed, healthy, uncomprehending faces of the younger ones, the touches of Catholic anti-Semitism, their fanatical hatred of female sexuality (though it was years before I could put a name to that), their physical intolerance. They differed from the school bullies, in a school where bullying was as organized as mealtimes, only in age and authority. The most shocking thing about boarding school for any sensitive child is the values of the aspirant middle classes, but Irish Catholicism adds an extra twist of the knife.

The landscape I loved with passion, because it meant escape.

but I could not read it. I thought the perfect valley and the woods below the school were natural, they had been there for ever. The Arcadian dark double lake was obviously put there on purpose, but I preferred to think of it as ancient. I was an Indian fighting his way through a swamp, or a soldier with a stick for a sword fighting across the bridge. The woods were a forest of fantasies. I was unable to distinguish the eighteenth-century buildings from the nineteenth, which at Prior Park is almost forgivable, because what was added in the nineteenth century was built as beautifully and in the same stone. I loved antiquity of all kinds because it was romantic and somehow unsullied by the Brothers. It was clear enough that the buildings had an old purpose and a magnificence of their own different in scale from Ruislip and the purposes of school; nothing could alter that, it was part of the place.

A stick of bombs nearly destroyed Prior Park altogether, at the end of the summer holidays of 1941 or 1942. It transformed the inside of one wing into a thrilling ruin. But most of that was soon repaired, and the essential images survived. Not a statue toppled from the arcades. The biggest alteration to Prior Park in my day was the steady eating away of the mounds that stood around the games fields behind the school, on the flat top of Combe Down Hill. Boys who hated games used to be drafted into a work force with pickaxes and wheelbarrows to demolish one terrestrial heaving after the other, to make more and more games fields. The mounds were lovely, and strictly out of bounds, because behind them ran the school wall, which was climbable. The mounds were no higher than twenty feet, but they were crowned with trees, and they had a wildness. We believed they were part of Offa's Dyke. Beyond the school grounds they ran on into Monument Wood, which was public, though it must once have belonged to Prior Park. The Monument was a Gothic folly, a carved stone tower standing alone in a field. It was ruinous and swathed in barbed wire and investigated only by cows.

I have no real idea what the mounds were, and the thought

of them now breeds in me a sadness and reluctance to find out. The easiest conjecture is that Ralph Allen had them thrown up when he built his house, but they lay well back out of sight, separated by a cricket field from the slopes above the mansion, as we called it. They were certainly not part of Offa's Dyke. Offa was an eighth-century King of Mercia, though I think as a schoolboy I imagined he was a West Saxon. His real Dyke, which is well preserved, and among the most awe-inspiring survivals of Dark Age Britain, was a practical barricade across mountainous and broken country to keep away the Welsh. Its southern extremity reaches the Bristol Channel somewhere near Chepstow. It runs many miles from north to south along the Welsh border, dominating the countryside to the west throughout its enormous length. The mounds above Prior Park dominated nothing but a cricket field.

If they were really the relic of some ancient defence wall, and it is hard to see what else they were, then they may have been built before the Romans came. Their purpose really remains as obscure as their date, and I take pleasure in that obscurity, and in their ragged sides and ruffled trees and the ditches full of darkness and old leaves. The voice and genius of a place may well speak silently and obscurely, after so many centuries. In all kinds of disorganized copses, and among mounds and heaps and quarry-spoil, people like me feel a lightening of the heart, a sharp and dog-like curiosity, a certain reverence for relics. I am sure that personally I owe the feeling to those sheltering bumps and tumps around the edge of the cricket-field. As for their true origin, it is likely enough or seems so now as I write, that at one time the encircling ramparts, which as I recall them surrounded the games fields on three sides, must once have had a fourth side, along the hill-top just above Prior Park. If so, the cricket field was once the centre of a prehistoric fortress of which we know nothing except that it dominated a valley above Bath.

That would not be the only time in the nineteenth century that ancient mounds had been levelled to make a cricket field.

The University Parks at Oxford used to be pleasantly studded with mounds: those were the relics of the civil war in the seventeenth century. Here and there on that side of Oxford, some relics of the relics do still exist, and long stretches of the city wall have survived here and there as boundary walls of colleges. Only a few years ago elm trees had to be cut down at my own college, St Catherine's, which lies towards the University Parks; we found that they were planted by the Corporation of Oxford at the restoration of Charles II, as part of a scheme to tidy up the battlefields of the civil war. It is quite possible that the mounds at Prior Park were no older. On the other hand, the *Anglo-Saxon Chronicle* records that in 577 AD Cuthwine and Ceawlin fought against the British at Deorham (which is now Dyrham, six miles north of Bath), and killed three kings, Coinmail, Condidan, and Farinmail, and took three chesters (three cities), Gloucester and Cirencester and Bath. The face of England has been terribly scratched and fought over. As a schoolboy I thought all these wars were unconnected and highly romantic. I did not see what they meant.

Going to Bath and back, often by car, did mean the beginnings of seeing England. The old Bath road from London shows you the Berkshire Downs. We used to stop for coffee, or in my case tonic water against car sickness, at the Bear at Hungerford; that was still an empty old coaching inn with wood fires and a cockatoo in the bar that said 'Goodbye darling' and 'Polly wants some whisky.' The second stop was Savernake Forest for a picnic. It was only the edge or the remnant of a forest, but an idyllic, pleasant place where we laughed a lot and dabbled in the stream for silver forks. I suppose there were fewer forests and woods left unfelled in England in the 1940s than ever before or since. Or were there fewer still when the famine for naval timber and industrial fuel was worst, a hundred years earlier? The National Forestry plantations had hardly begun in 1939, and where they did exist people complained of their ugliness. The difference of appearance in the last thirty years, as those trees have come to maturity, is as if the sea had covered the land. As it did once. The chalk downs owe their perfect rhythms, their steep wave-like sides and all their majestic shapeliness to the sea. They were once the floor of a warm and rather shallow inlet of the ocean. Their typical forms are as much determined by the ocean as a gull's form by the flowing air and the hull design of a fishing boat by the motion of sea-water.

I did have some sense of the age of rocks and the different kinds of countryside. My passion was mostly reserved for a hill in Dorset called Golden Cap where I scrambled like a baby on its mother, but the tall, brambly, vivid green hills and deep combes of inland Dorset seemed to me then less remarkable, because they were not unlike the country round Prior Park. Now that comes back in dreams, though never alas as a continuous landscape, only intense flashes of memory, a beckoning orchard, a huge plane tree on the turn of a path, or an overgrown slope on private land where we were once shot at by an angry landowner; huge cloudy skies, smells of apples and wild garlic. Of the history of landscape I was innocent. I was for the British against the Romans, for the Romans against all invaders, for the English (how did they come to be one people?) against the Normans, for the Anglo-Normans against all Europe. It was always 1940 in my imagination. *Puck of Pook's Hill* was only an extension of Walter Scott. It never occurred to me that tribal war or even class war in the past had done any harm.

The most impressive ancient monument I had ever seen then, and the most thrilling landscape I could imagine ever seeing, was Stonehenge, and second to that the White Horse. Both of them, as even a child could see, were awe-inspiring because of their simplicity and isolation. They had no relation to the rest of the world. They communicated only with rain-clouds and mist or the light-blue sky, and with acres and acres of sheep-cropped grass. The other day, someone published a neat and convincing demonstration of the date of the White

Horse, by relating it to the horses on the coinage of the Dark Ages. I had noticed that similarity as a child, because I hoarded ancient coins as my brother hoarded stamps. But most of the Roman coins that came my way were only late Roman and in battered condition; indeed the same can be said of most of the remains of Roman Britain. By comparison the Anglo-Saxon coins in the junk shops in those days seemed wonderfully ancient; one could see without clear reasoning that they stood for an England more ancient than the Romans, a place of horses and forests and the moon, in which the tidy head of the Empress Faustina, who wore her hair in a bun like a New England school-mistress, was an alien object, however beautiful.

Stonehenge had the primacy by the limitless extent of unambitious grazing ground which still in those days surrounded it. Salisbury Plain had such an air of solemn antiquity as nothing human could have. Unenclosed, prehistoric landscape is very rare in Britain, but in my childhood Stonehenge still gave at least some impression of it. In living memory it was haunted by wild bustards, oddest looking of birds. A lot of land all over the country was never ploughed until 1939 or 1945, and since that time the invention of chemical fertilizers has transformed British landscape. The infestation of motor cars and buses had hardly started before the war; during the war little traffic except a few military convoys could be seen. The dogcarts and ponytraps and open carriages now in the Northleach museum were still in private hands then. In fact they were brought back into use in 1939; as a young girl my wife used to ride in them. I have known old grooms turned chauffeurs who used to hiss as they polished their cars; they were alive thirty years ago. It will seem pedantic to elderly readers to point these things out, but young people do not know them. When I was a boy, the Victorian age appeared to us mythical, yet it was less long ago than 1939 is today. Few things in my lifetime have altered as unexpectedly as Stonehenge.

The texture of the stones in that desert and their magnitude, the huge scale and lack of obvious purpose of the whole affair, the incoherence of its ruins, and the levels and slow heaves of the plain itself, still make an impression. The monolithic pillars have a kind of harmony, like very heavy dancing. One can see why the Normans thought they were brought 'by giants out of Afric', or assembled here by the wizard Merlin. But the fact that we now know the mountain in south-west Wales where they were quarried adds still more to their fascination. The founding father of all geography, the Greek Hekataios, kinsman of Herodotos the historian, knew before Socrates was born that in the centre of the island of Britain stood a circular temple of the sun. And yet no one knows exactly the purpose or the origin of Stonehenge. It was not in use in classical times, or not in its first use. It stands there infinitely enduring, with its shoulders hunched. The Norman Welsh priest Gerald of Barry conjectured that it might be a war memorial for the defeated British of the Dark Ages. In my mind it does stand as one, but in its youth it was more like a British Parthenon. I do not think there is any other monument in the world of so great natural and at the same time so great human grandeur.

Little as any boy of my generation understood the landscape, I understood the Irish even less. The two ignorances are closely connected. We were taught nothing at school about the pre-Roman British, and little about the pre-Norman English. We never pondered the slowness of the Angle and Saxon invasions, or the tragic and noble resistance of the old inhabitants of this island. We were led to believe that Christian Wessex unified England, never that kings of Wessex owed allegiance to an over-king in Northumbria, never that Mercia was the greatest of the Anglo-Saxon kingdoms, never the extent of the conquest and settlement by the Danes. We never knew the importance of the North or felt how the West was a sanctuary and a refuge of the old British race. We never thought about Viking sculpture. We supposed the *Book of Kells* was an isolated mystery. It certainly never occurred to us that the earliest foundations of democracy were due in England to racial diversity and the impotence of central government againt the provinces.

When it was mentioned, Ireland was pictured to us as an impregnable natural fortress with a pure and austere civilization of its own. And yet Yeats and the Celtic twilight had left the Brothers untouched. The poems they knew by Yeats were *Innisfree* and one about a priest. I puzzled as a little boy over *Innisfree*. Nine beanrows and a hive for the honeybee seemed a meagre provision for the poet. But it was a beautiful poem and I felt strongly its longing to escape. When Yeats died I was truly shocked. I was only nine, and I had never heard of any other living poets. I thought maybe there were no poets left alive any more. The real Ireland was as remote to me as the real Yeats. I had never heard of Ulster except in books of mythology. What I grew up to discover was that civil war and tribal war are the worst things in the world. The English treatment of the Irish was carried over and adapted from English treatment of the Welsh and Norman treatment of Welsh and English alike. The English have never treated any other nation so badly, because the Irish were the closest. Those attitudes to savage or wild people that had such a terrible effect in India and in America were simply carried over from dealing with Ireland.

The Brothers were not profound scholars or original thinkers, nor were they liberals, and the results of archaeology were scarcely available to them. Their task, which they treated with determination, was to push us through simple examinations. The theories we were taught about every subject except for Ireland and Catholicism were the received theories. Their personal culture had strong roots in the nineteenth century, as most people's did then. The older ones who taught me were brought up in Victorian Ireland: they were already teachers of thirty in 1916. Such precise political events as the Easter Rebellion were not mentioned: all stories of martyrdoms and English oppression faded into a single haze from Cromwell to the Black and Tans, to whom I could not have put a date. Of the civil war that followed Irish independence, never a word.

None of those who taught me gave any evidence of reading Gaelic literature. Their literary horizon was bound by one year's syllabus or another's.

Still, quite a lot of Latin was on the syllabus, so some interest was shown in the Romans. The excellence and occasional subtlety of Caesar's prose was lost on me as it always is on schoolboys. He seemed like an endless, tedious television action serial, in which the British always lost. I did at one point try Josephus, because that at least had some Jews in it, but Whiston's translation was too tedious. The dust had got into the ink-bottle, the tedium had yellowed the pages. It is better to read things in the original. My first attempt at Virgil revealed to my puzzled young eyes only a poet who embedded wonderful single lines in long tracts of heavy going; he seemed no more difficult as a poet than Milton, and rather similar in tone, but it shames me to think how little I could make of the *Aeneid*. I think it was the story I disliked. But classical Bath spread out against the opposite sky. The Roman baths lay tranquilly stinking at the foot of our hill. The famous medicinal water tasted like camel's foot-rot, it was a well-known dare to drink a glass of it. Every St Patrick's day, in the first of the March sun, the whole junior school would troop down the hill to be taken round the Roman baths.

Part of this often repeated visit was underground, most of it was tedious. One was shown the beginners' pool and the cold pool and the contemptibly low stone diving board worn away by bare feet. One was never allowed to swim. The best moment was the waterspring itself. That smelt nauseating, but it was undoubtedly hot water: the Waters of the Sun, *Aquae Sulis*, Bath. The water poured down from a rockface like a waterfall. To observe it you entered a small room, a sort of balcony. The game was to stay there as long as you possibly could, because if you stayed there long enough your white, stiff, idiotic Eton collar, worn outside the jacket collar, would lose its starch and relax into the texture of a handkerchief. The Brothers treated this ritual as not permissible, because we had to be outwitted into respectability, but as having its place in the universe, much like the Roman bath. Irish boys wore shamrock, which wilted.

Everything that can be done to a subject people was done by the English to the Irish, and everything that a colonized, victimized people becomes the southern Irish in their turn became. The splendid intransigence and integrity of Ulster people is another matter. This has nothing to do with religion: if the English had stayed Catholic, the Irish would surely have gone Protestant. The character of the colonized is the same world-wide: the same dishonesty, vengefulness, irony and unreliability crop up in the characters of the Slav hero Marko under the Turks, the Greek Karaghiozis in the shadow-puppet plays, an even more advanced case, and in the old complaints of English colonial governors. That remarkable old man Sir John Davies, a lawyer who served in Ireland under Elizabeth I, wrote 'A Discovery of the True Causes why Ireland was never entirely subdued' until the end of her reign. He blamed English extortion and oppression, rapacious landlords and royal parsimony.

'So as this extreme Extortion and Oppression hath been the true cause of the idleness of this *Irish* Nation. Lastly, this Oppression did of force and necessity make the *Irish* a crafty People: for such as are oppressed and live in slavery, are ever put to their shifts.'

Davies was concerned to argue down the libellous opinion then current in Europe that the British had neglected to conquer Ireland for deliberate reasons, 'thinking it more fit to continue that Realm in Barbarism'. Of the barbarism, the physical and moral backwardness, he had no doubt. Ulster was desolate for lack of a stabilizing law of inheritance. The murder of an Irishman was not, under Irish law, which the English applied, a felony or a capital crime. The Irish not being 'of free blood', their murder was expiated with a fine. 'I omit their common repudiation of their wives; their promiscuous generation of Children; their neglect of lawful Matrimony; their uncleanness in Apparel, Diet, and Lodging; and their contempt and scorn of all things necessary for the civil life of man.' In fact he thought about them as white people thought until yesterday about Africans. Thank God the midnight of that yesterday has chimed.

What is far more odd is that with York and Lancaster united, with Scotland and England under one crown, with 'the work of God through a woman' accomplished now through Elizabeth as once through the Virgin Mary (that is how he saw it) and Ireland conquered, he prophesied a peaceful, concordant future. 'The Clock of the Civil Government is now well set, and all the Wheels thereof do move in Order; the Strings of this Irish Harp, which the Civil Magistrates do finger, are all in tune.' So much for the wisdom of lawyers. For the character of the Irish as the Elizabethans saw it, we can summon an earlier and perhaps more interesting witness. Edmund Campion, who later became a saint and a martyr, wrote in his youth, when he still half hoped for preferment at court, a history of Ireland dedicated to the Earl of Leicester. He wrote in the house of James Stanihurst, Recorder of Dublin, but the English authorities in England did not think him sound. Still, the liveliness and brilliance of his style, and his humorous sympathies, do not disguise his colonial assumptions. His voice is that of a young gallant in Shakespeare, where the voice of Sir John Davies is that of Polonius, or at times of Justice Shallow.

Campion wrote his book in under ten weeks, ramming together most of the early material with the help of young Richard Stanihurst, a young man as unsound as he was, a splendidly crabbed and perverse translator of Virgil, from whatever old writings they could find, a task 'full of unsavoury toil'. Campion failed to learn Irish as he wished; he failed even to find a competent interpreter. But wherever he speaks freely, his words are magical. 'Ireland lieth aloof in the Western Ocean. In proportion it resembleth an egg, blunt and plain on the sides, not reaching forth to sea, in nooks and elbows of land, as Britain doth . . . Horses they have of pace easy, in running wonderful swift.' He means Arab horses from Spain.

'Eagles are well known to breed here, but neither so big nor so many as books tell.' What land the English controlled had been deforested. 'The air is wholesome, not altogether cleare and subtle as ours of England. They are not without wolves, and greyhounds to hunt them, bigger of bone and limb than a colt.' So far, so good.

'Clear men they are of skin and hue, but of themselves careless and bestial.' The women are 'suffered from their infancy to grow at will', that is, shockingly uncorseted. The men 'have now left their Saffron, and learn to wash their shirts, four or five times in a year . . . Shamrocks, Watercresses, Roots, and other Herbs they feed upon: Oatmeal and Butter they cram together. Aquavitae . . . by quarts and pottles. Their kine they let blood, which grown to a jelly they bake and overspread with Butter, and so eat it in lumps.' They follow their dead to the grave 'with howlings and barbarous outcries', whence comes the proverb 'to weep Irish'. 'The people are thus inclined; religious, franke, amorous, irefull, sufferable, of paines infinite, very glorious, many sorcerers, excellent horsemen, delighted with Wars; great alms-givers, passing in hospitalitie; the lewder sort both Clerks and Laymen are sensual and loose to lechery above measure. The same being virtuously bred up or reformed, are such mirrors of holiness and austerity, that other Nations retain but a show or shadow of devotion in comparison of them . . . Greedy of praise they be, and fearful of dishonour.'

Campion is both a prophecy of his future self and a kind of Shakespeare: his English are Prospero and his Irish are Caliban. 'The very English of birth, conversant with the brutish sort of that people, become degenerate in short space, and are quite altered into the worst rank of Irish rogues.' The Irish are terribly vengeful. 'In some corners of the land they use a damnable superstition, leaving the right arms of their infant males unchristened (as they termed it) to the intent it might give a more ungracious and deadly blow.' When the English wanted to send a sherriff into Fermanagh, so Davies records, the Maguire, who ruled Fermanagh then, accepted him at once, but asked what price of compensation the English set on him. 'Your Sherriff shall be welcome to me, but let me know his *Ericke*, or the price of his head, aforehand, that if my people cut it off, I may cut the *Ericke* upon the county.'

The Irish problem, which the Irish with some justice call the English problem, was essentially in existence by the 1560s. Gerald of Barry, a cousin of those Fitz-Geralds and Fitz-Stephens who as Sir John Davies put it 'first brake the Ice, with a party of Three hundred and ninety Men' under Henry II, recorded its beginnings in the terms of his own generation. He put it as a prophecy into the mouth of the Archbishop of Cashel. 'Although our people are very barbarous, uncivilized, and savage, nevertheless they have never put out their hands against the saints of God. But now a people has come to the kingdom which knows how, and is accustomed, to make martyrs. From now on Ireland will have its martyrs, just like other countries.' It is curious in more ways than one that Gerald of Barry wrote of the view between England (more exactly Scotland) and Ireland that 'the view from this side is rather clear, that from the other, over such a distance, is more vague'. Morally, the opposite is true. The opinion of victims of every kind always has a special truth, which is preferable to the Olympian half-truths of the victimizers. By this I mean to defend both my own truth against the Olympian views of my schoolmasters and their Irish truth against the English. That is because after half a century of experience I believe in no justice on earth except poetic justice; and neither, I believe, does God.

Of course the Irish used to be barbarous, both for better and worse. The schooling of bards in the traditional techniques of poetry, an austere and deeply searching process to which I imagine that early Irish monasticism, the discipline of Iona and of Lindisfarne, owed a good deal, continued in Ireland into the eighteenth century. The last of the Scottish Gaelic bards had to cross over to Ireland to be schooled. That is one aspect of barbarism. 'The tongue is sharp and sententious,' says Campion, 'wherefore their common Jesters, Bards, and Rhymers, are said to delight passingly those that conceive the grace and propriety of the tongue . . . They esteem their Poets . . . One office in the house of great men is a tale-teller, who bringeth his Lord on sleep, with tales vain and frivolous.' My own favourite of those he records is that of the priest who took up a collection in villages for curing Saint Patrick's sore head, which Saint Peter had recently broken with the keys, because Saint Patrick was trying to argue a poor hard-swearing Irishman into Heaven.

Before Campion's time but not so early as Gerald of Barry, in the reign of Henry VIII a Greek traveller usually called Nicander, a diplomat who turned soldier and fought for Henry against the Scots in the regiment of Thomas of Argos, composed in his own language an account of these islands which deserves to be better known. The Irish 'are tall, fair-complexioned, and rather light-haired, wearing much hair on their heads and having a shaggy beard'. They were nearly naked, they were archers, they could run with horses or with dogs. It sounds as if someone had met them out hunting. They were wonderful throwers, just like the Brothers, and 'engage in battle hand to hand' with tremendous courage, like the German tribes in Caesar and Tacitus. The civilized ones wore 'garments extending to the feet, in barbaric fashion. And towards their own females they conduct themselves with too great simplicity, inasmuch as sometimes they have sexual intercourse with them in public, and think it no shame.' Perhaps that was what frightened the Brothers. 'The flat parts of Ireland are boggy, whence the air is often misty, as exhalations arise from the morasses.' A large part of England was as boggy as that when the Romans left it. Throughout the Middle Ages, it was slowly and painfully drained. The landscape of Prior Park was the crown of many centuries of anonymous toil and restless refinement of technique: just as much so as the poetry of Milton and of Pope.

The miserable inner world of decreases of happiness, and of

education becoming worse as one grew to need it more, is hard to relate to the physical atmosphere of Combe Down. The truth to grasp is that Prior Park as a place was victoriously perfect, and the joy I got from it has remained, while the misery disintegrated to rags and tatters. The worst it did was to leave me in spirit unteachable, almost intractable, difficult to handle, what the French call a *mauvais sujet*: not a bad thing for a poet, and curiously not at all unusual for a Jesuit, which was my future and twenty-eight years of my life. Can one be pressurized into a sense of vocation or calling? So far as I can tell, I was not.

What I wanted to become I chose freely, and the sense of tranquil inner freedom has never deserted me in any crisis. Is that, as people claim, the private territory of God in the human soul, or am I right to associate it strongly with a landscape? The landscape of Prior Park was my father's mysterious gift. It educated me as the Brothers could not have done. Even the most secret hunger for sanctity that lurked or still lurks in me, as I can admit nowadays, under many layers of perverse and romantic disguises, has something in common not with the Brothers but with old Irish hermits on sea-rocks and lake islands: the Inner Farne, the Brass Rock, Ynys Gybi, Flatholm, Belcinac. When I revisited Prior Park a few years ago, the woods were mothy, and the Brothers seemed lonelier and more unkempt than they used to be. All the same, if I had to choose between the Irish clergy (Ireland nearly at its worst) and their English equivalent, my loyalty would still be expressed in the words of the old song one of the Brothers used to sing in his most cheerful moods. 'Up to theology, down to conchology, Father O'Flynn would make hay of them all.'

The English had been wrong to despise Irish culture. On that night I mentioned at the Dublin festival, one of the translations that was read was the *Keen for Art O'Leary*. I had never heard of it. Its power, its grandeur and its sadness are like the *Iliad*. Hearing it for the first time was the single most moving experience of that kind I have ever had. In a way I am still reeling from the impact; I am seldom able to reread the *Keen for Art O'Leary* without tears. Most late Gaelic poetry has a thin and trailing quality: it is worlds away from the old epics, as the Brothers were worlds away from the old saints. In the *Keen* a world of feeling like that of the *Iliad* is still alive. The poem was composed in 1773, but not written down. It was remembered and recited by illiterate people, and recovered from the memories of Cork fishermen at the end of the nineteenth century. Surely this was the greatest poem written in these islands, indeed in all Europe, in the whole eighteenth century. Goethe and Wordsworth would have thought so, and so would Dryden and probably Pope. These claims will not seem extraordinary to those who know the four hundred short lines of Eilis Dillon's translation.

Arthur O'Leary was shot by pursuing soldiers on 4 May 1773, and buried at Kilnamartin in unconsecrated ground; his body was moved that autumn to the ruined monastery at Kilcrea. We have his English epitaph, which was written, as his *Keen* was, by his widow, Eibhlin Dhubh, Dark Eileen. She was the last of the old Irish poets. Writing in English she sounds like any talented major or minor poet of the day.

> Lo! Arthur Leary, generous, handsome, brave,
> Slain in his bloom, lies in this humble grave.
> Died May 4th, 1773, Aged 26 years.

Her father was Domhnall Mor O'Connell, builder of Derrynane house, on the south-west tip of Kerry, who had twenty-two children. Her mother was a famous poet in her own time, and the family were patrons of wandering poets. They kept tutors; one of the children grew up to be a courtier of Maria Theresa, and Daniel O'Connell was a kinsman. Eileen was married off at fifteen to a wealthy old man who died in six months. She fell in love with Arthur O'Leary when she saw him through a window as he rode through the town of Macroom. She was twenty-four and he was twenty-one, a

Captain in the Austrian Army. The family disliked his marrying Eileen. He wore a sword, illegal for Catholics (which neatly defined the Irish), and he offended Abraham Morris, High Sherriff of Cork, by beating the Sherriff's horse at Macroom races. The Sherriff appealed to the law against any Catholic owning a horse worth more than five pounds. Arthur O'Leary defied him, and he was outlawed. He was spotted not long afterwards by a traitor called John Cooney, pursued by the garrison soldiers, and shot down. He was as much the victim of England, if not more so, as those Irish lords whose death Campion recorded, failing perhaps to foresee his own.

'To whom FitzGerald yielded, and was sent into England, where he with his Uncles, and other Principals of the conspiracy were afterwards drawn, hanged and quartered at Tyburn.'

CHAPTER THREE

A Tower of Sand

Lock up this summer in a casket of hay
In a tower of sand in the wind's embrace . . .
Anne Pennington

MY FAVOURITE CHARACTER at school was Mr Haskell, the groundsman, who farmed a few stony patches of field and took part in the mound-levelling campaigns of every winter. He built the beacon that blazed up higher than the woods on the night the war ended in Europe. That was pure beech and oak; there was nothing left of it by morning but white woodash with cattle sleeping in the ashes to keep warm. Mr Haskell was an old Wiltshire quarryman; his face was tanned and lined, he wore dignified, old-fashioned clothes, a waistcoat and gaiters usually, and he had a huge silver turnip of a watch for keeping work parties at work until the last second of the last minute. His voice had a sharper burr to it than the local Somerset accent. He was kind to me as a child, not very often or very kind, but it was enough that he was never unkind, and he never expected one to be good at pickaxing. I was eleven then, and hardly able to lift a pickaxe. Mr Haskell told us bloodcurdling stories about working conditions and low pay in the quarries in his boyhood.

That was long ago, so I thought, in another age. I had little precise sense of money or class. Sixpence seemed a lot of money to me. My attitude to working-class children was bright-eyed, mouse-like curiosity mingled with envy because they seemed freer than I was. They went to bed later. They worked on coal lorries on a Saturday. They had chewing gum. When my mother once pointed out that a boy I brought home seemed embarrassed by us and suggested I ought not to make him such a friend, I was affronted, not ashamed. I wagged my tail to everyone I met and called all grown men Sir, as my father did, unless they were family friends. I was snobbish about the country as opposed to the town, and that was all. People like Mr Haskell were my gods. I liked their voices and their language and their huge hands and sober experience. I admired their skills beyond measure. Carpenter's tools are a very early memory. Once I possessed an adze, though I never learnt how to use one. Using a scythe for a few afternoons has been one of the most joyful satisfactions in fifty years of life: just holding those long tongues in balance and letting them swish. The pleasure of scything is like that of boating; the scyther in the grass is just as much drowned in the physical sensations of meadows as the rower is in those of river water and riverbanks. Old countrymen like Mr Haskell had at least a hundred traditional skills they used in any one year, but I knew that young men in the city have only one.

This kind of hero-worship of servants used to be widespread, but I suppose it was always selective. Some of the servants were quite grotesque: I remember an Irish maid at Prior Park with a paper-white face and a ginger wig, and a terrible old woman cleaner the boys called Mrs Pee-rag, and some fearful, spitting old men with yellow moustaches. Grotesque adults struggling for an ignoble living did give one a sense of another class, but they seemed to be left over from a dead world in which the depression of the 1930s tailed off into the slum novels of Dickens. I was more terrified than I knew at that time by Dickens, and by the loneliness and mania of his characters. I never understood what it was in Dickens that was like a darkness calling to a darkness until I talked about him to Peter Shaffer. The first sentence of some long forgotten chapter, 'the mist was up on the marshes' sends a shiver up my spine to this day. Once at Prior Park we saw a documentary film about London slums and slum clearance that gave me nightmares. The sheer cold hopelessness of the new buildings was almost worse than the rats' nests of the old ones. One knew that the cheerful film voice was not going to cure anything. Nothing could wipe out such a past.

My snobbery about the country, the wilder and the more unexplored the better, had got to the point where if the old Indian army sergeant had tried to explain Irish troubles to me as he did to a friend of mine in the fifties, 'The ordinary people is all right, but it's them wild tribes in the hills,' my sympathy would have gone to the hills. *Stalky and Co.* was a book I understood all too well.

My last two years of school were spent at Beaumont, beside the fatherly, dull Thames on the edge of Windsor Great Park. I went there to learn Greek. It was certainly a rest, after the other place, and a time of pleasure. Little by little I relaxed. I learnt Greek, read poetry, and experimented at making friends of my own age. We tried drink and talked about sex. I remember myself then as tiresome, and constantly changing, though on the whole for the better because relaxed has to mean better. The Thames was an old friend who always had something new to say. I became deeply fond of Windsor Castle and all its woods and rides. We hung out of our windows on summer evenings to hear the last bugle calls floating over the oak trees as if the year were 1911.

What moved me so much about Windsor Park, as we ran through it on winter afternoons and rambled about in it chasing rabbits on summer Sundays, was its beautiful tameness: the easy, luxurious slopes and grass walks between seas of bracken and huge oak trees and chestnuts. I had no idea then of its real wildness late into the eighteenth century. I never knew it used to be full of Robin Hoods. I knew Shelley had a cottage at Bishopsgate, but not that Pope was born in the park. I did know of Herne the Hunter, because I had an autographed copy of the novel about him from a second-hand shop at Bath. But I knew nothing at all of the persistent rebelliousness and independence of the Windsor foresters so late in history. I had never even heard of Peacock's wonderful piece of reporting, *The Last Day of Windsor Forest*, when regiments of cavalry in extended lines rounded up and took away the Windsor deer. To me it was just another empty paradise to roam around, with a strong smell of leaves at every time of the year.

Since what I am struggling to record is the growth of a boy's consciousness of places in Britain, of landscapes and country-sides, and the petrified, dead conflict that they embody, then also the consequences of that conflict in all our history down to this day, it may be important to say a little more about the extension of views I underwent at Beaumont between the ages of fifteen and seventeen. In the first place I came to put a higher, perhaps too high a value on national institutions. 'Bow, bow, ye lower middle classes!' Gilbert and Sullivan command. I bowed, I was a romantic monarchist with Jacobite leanings, differing only in date from the child in Sinister Street. Windsor Castle, with its library and galleries, the Palace and the Houses of Parliament and Westminster Abbey were visible and solemn monuments, they were no longer mirages trembling on the exhalations of an Irish bog.

When I was about sixteen, I went by mistake, not having realized it was voluntary, to a cadet corps camp on Aldershot racecourse. Round and round the long racecourse a Lieute-nant-Colonel of a Parachute Regiment, the fifth I think, rode his horse, attended by a pair of dogs: were they retrievers or greyhounds? At sunset, as the mosquitoes began to bite more seriously, and the pink and yellow sandbanks of cloud spread themselves across the heavens, a band of kilted highlanders played bagpipes and marched and counter-marched. *Over the sea to Skye* is under those circumstances irresistible. The sergeant instructors were the kindest of men. They called you sonny, and gave you sweet advice as if you really were their son. 'You hold it like this sonny.' 'Look son, don't never volunteer for one of them, don't never go in tanks. Look where them shots have gone right through it.' I had never in my life until that time been treated by adults on such almost equal terms. I had met parachutists a few years earlier, when they camped on the cricket field at Prior Park just before Arnhem, just before they died. Those soldiers had been sensationally glamorous and friendly. But this was a new dimension. As a boy it made me want to be an officer, a predictably boyish reaction. Since then, I have wondered whether, merging with Mr Haskell and the Rigg family, that summer lies at the roots of what I now call socialism.

And of course as you grow up people become more real to you, they have more social and personal depth. I remember being crazy as a boy at Beaumont about writing a novel, so important to me that I never wrote down more than a few pages of it, for fear I might spoil it. The image that was the core of this fiction was some cyclists, a club of them riding racing-bicycles, coming from some unknown part of the desert of south London. They came in from the rain with their clothes steaming, for a cup of tea in some tiny teashop on the approaches to Staines. Or so I imagined. The tables had metal edges. The tea was foul but sweet. It seemed to me then terribly important that this was all right, their experience satisfied them as mine might or might not give me pleasure. The moral of my novel was that any trivial thing, even a bus ticket, was ground for rejoicing. But theirs was a world as alien as I could possibly imagine. They were people to whom one would never speak, to whom no one else at school would want to speak (or so I suppose I felt). Was this the influence of H. G. Wells? Was it Mr Polly or Mr Kipps, or was it something out of Chesterton? In one way or another, we do mysteriously advance by reading; we advance in regiments of a generation at a time, even though as boys we never know one another.

In my last year at school, I had infantile paralysis, which ended my dreams of the Parachute Regiment with merciful absence of argument. But how did I come to join the Jesuits? It was an easy decision at the time. My mother had been keen on my transferring to Beaumont in the first place, because I frightened her I might take up with a dotty religious order she had never heard of, devoting itself to proselytizing the Jews. My father favoured the same transfer for simpler reasons, because he could never understand what the Brothers were on about, and because they botched my brother's future and neglected mine. Myself, I just wanted to learn Greek, because Oscar Wilde had said the New Testament in Greek was the most beautiful book in the world, and I believed him. He was right, too. The Jesuits at Beaumont not only knew Greek, but they smelt of wisdom and pipe tobacco. But I did not like them at all as much as the tailor, Albert, who had a walrus brown moustache, and knew all boys and all old boys however old by their laundry number. Or as Percy, the RSM, a smart little soldier with waxed moustaches, who called us 'You pretty ruddy darlings.' Still, some of the Jesuits were admirable, and one was a genius. My special teacher was Mr Brinkman, who had advanced views about Aeschylus and Bach, and told us to read *Horizon* and Evelyn Waugh. The Rector of Beaumont was a saint I suppose, of a rather Anglican than Catholic kind. He attended garden parties at Windsor on a rattling bicycle, in clerical morning dress of pea-green antiquity. The genius was Christopher Devlin, a poet and writer I still cannot think of without sighing from mere affection. As a schoolmaster, he was a volcano. In his private character he recalled Shakespearean comedy, but in the classroom he was sometimes King Lear.

When the moment came for becoming a Jesuit, I was interviewed first of all by saturnine Father D'Arcy. I confessed that what I liked was the cloak and dagger, or cloak and crucifix aspect of Elizabethan Jesuits, but I also respected my schoolmasters. Had he known what Prior Park was like by contrast, he would not have felt flattered or surprised by that. I liked D'Arcy greatly. He gave the impression of a real human being thinking, and that was new to me. And I liked his interest in death, which I shared, and his innocent enthusiasm both for works of art and for human beings of uneven merit. I am grateful that he accepted me: I would have languished in an office. You had to have four other examiners. One has dissolved in past time. One was the headmaster, who asked me questions about sex to which I automatically replied with a very straight bat indeed. One was Chris Devlin, who was shaving, half an hour before lunch. He spent the interview gesturing with a shaving brush and looking up books explaining with glee how being a Jew I would need an entire legal process at Rome before I could even apply. This thrilled him, he thought it was so silly and peculiar, it really delighted him as a fact about life. The last examiner was a scruffy-looking Lancashireman with an accent, dandruff and bad breath, patron of stage scene-painters and incapables, some of them my friends. He presided over my first awkward attempts to learn rowing. Now he warned me, as he rolled his own filthy-looking cigarette, how I might hate the noviceship, because boys from grammar schools sometimes made a noise when they ate. This bizarre information has worried me ever since, and I have been listening for thirty-five years, but I have never yet been able to determine social class by decibels of munching.

So it was goodbye to Windsor, and goodbye to the pretence to be a gentleman and to many other budding poses. The ugly duckling need never grow up to be a swan. From 1948 until 1976 I can reasonably describe myself as attempting and finally attaining a more or less classless condition, in which I was outside the rat race, a benign observer and private friend of mankind. As for the world I left, my vision of the future England at the time of the Queen's coronation was not unlike Pope's vision in his long poem *Windsor Forest*, which he wrote to celebrate the Treaty of Utrecht, to welcome in an age of peace and concord.

> Till the freed *Indians* in their native Groves
> Reap their own Fruits, and woo their Sable Loves,
> *Peru* once more a Race of Kings behold,
> And other *Mexicos* be roofed with Gold.

Unfortunately the Treaty of Utrecht, which was intended to produce peace, freedom, and equality by opening the seas of America to the British, led in reality to the worst and last chapters in the history of the slave trade. Even at home on the banks of the Thames the eighteenth century as it progressed reversed the beautiful prophecy which Pope had put into the mouth of that river:

> Safe on my shore each unmolested Swain
> Shall tend the Flocks, or reap the bearded Grain;
> The shady Empire shall retain no Trace
> Of War or Blood, but in the Sylvan Chase,
> The Trumpets sleep, while cheerful Horns are blown . . .

It is true that fox-hunting flourished, but the trumpets did not sleep. For more than a century after Pope's lifetime, enclosures and oppressions and rural poverty crushed the English peasants worse than they had done in his day. There is of course a clear relation between foreign wars and an empire that extended far beyond his 'shady Empire' of Windsor Forest, and the starving and ill-treated population of this country. The history of exploitation cannot be isolated into one island or barricaded away into the oriental distance; we are interconnected, we have all learnt that by now. Nelson's ships sailed into the Bay of Naples with British sailors hanging by the neck in their rigging. In the snowy fields of eighteenth-century winters, children of five and six were out before dawn picking stones and scaring crows. I knew an old man in Windsor whose grandfather was hanged from the clock tower of the castle for stealing an animal in the Great Park. That was under Victoria.

The terrible nature of our real history became apparent to me only very slowly, but I did at once, in the autumn of my eighteenth year, discover a new world of human beings. Jesuit novices, particularly in those years just after the war, were a mixed lot in every way, and numerous too. Many were demobilized soldiers. The course lasted two years, and I believe at one time there were fifty or sixty of us together, though no more than twenty or so a year survived to the end. We came together on the given day, in September with elm leaves and chestnut leaves yellowing, to a pretty chalk-white eighteenth-century house, a more modest but better designed Beaumont, overlooking Richmond Park. It lay among huge sleepy grounds, with orchards and pastures and pigsties and enormous walled gardens, as if we were still deep in the country. In winter the deer came up from the park to be fed at the kitchen door. Roehampton was a tiny village with two or three shops. Heath and common stretched away in every direction. The continuous noise of traffic was not audible at Roehampton until the fifties. You could hear the fall of a leaf or the footsteps of a squirrel in the suburbs of London.

It was in these unrecallable conditions, in this strange wonderland, that I got to know my first coalminer and university lecturer and Prussian nobleman and bank clerk and lower-deck sailor, on terms of more intimacy and equality than even military service at its luckiest could have offered. I had never before known who really lived in the North; now I could make friends with a dozen Lancashiremen and Scotsmen, and even stranger to me, people from other parts of the London suburbs that seemed as distant as Delhi. We spent about half our time doing the kind of jobs servants must have done in enormous houses a hundred years ago. We washed up in wooden sinks, we drew beer from the barrel, a weak and sour brew milder than mild that poor workmen used to buy once and no one makes anymore. We swept with wet sawdust and polished with bumpers, heavy weights that swivelled on the end of long broomsticks. We dealt with mangelwurzels and turnips. My least favourite job was emptying tureens of cold porridge, my favourite one was taking swill to the pigs. They were looked after by an elderly pigman called Dick Wernham, a very small cockney in a cap who used to kiss them on the snout.

The sheer old-fashionedness of the house at Roehampton is hard to describe today. Its gardens then were like some mothy backwater of Kew or Windsor, vast and silent. The house was in some ways like a monastery or the most austere of schools, with strange taboos and special ways of behaving that attached to the calender, the hours of the day, every hole and corner and bend of a gallery. The design of the building was fine, but by my time it was much cluttered with life-size holy statues all made of painted plaster. Some of them showed saints in extravagant attitudes of devotion. The gravel walks and the trees outside gave life an Edwardian air. On the whole, the place was well kept up, but as if there existed only the scurrying servants (us) with their mysterious routines, some senior servants (the elderly priests) whom we seldom saw, and no family at all, no owner. To say that Jesuit houses of that kind lacked a family touch or a woman's touch is to put it mildly. What they lacked was common humanity. Most of us were too much preoccupied with inward religion, rather a new and tricky matter for recent ex-schoolboys, to notice that at the time.

Maybe I should say more about those two years. The religious training, which was equally new to all of us, was a factor that made us spiritually extremely private and respecters of privacy. Into certain marginal areas of religion, jokes intruded which we nursed in common. For instance we were given ridiculous little string whips to beat ourselves. I suppose we tried to take this seriously in private, but when our eyes met we dissolved into profane laughter on the subject. I have the strong impression that most people made little use of these amazing aids to recollection in later life. Myself, I am afraid that I reported with a deadpan face that whipping gave me a sexual satisfaction. I have never heard anything forbidden more quickly. But that was years later, when I felt free enough to play around with the system. The aim of the Jesuit training is to produce a perfect inner freedom, a conscious freedom in which God, life, death, oneself and the world and the Crucifixion of Christ, are all tranquilly and completely accepted. The theory is that to serve Christ, to become a saint, a person needs only to be set free: freedom and the operation of grace make a heaven even of earth. It will be seen that this theory has paradoxes, and that the training may be more successful or less successful according to the individuals concerned. In my case if it succeeded at all, it took seventeen years to do so.

What it did accomplish, almost equally slowly, was to make me a poet and a kind of scholar. I was set free to read on and on in many unlikely sections of libraries. I was driven by something close to boredom, as many English Jesuits have been, to the near observation of nature, and by something like frustration to an intensity of vision. The obituary for Gerard Manley Hopkins in the privately circulated English Jesuit magazine spoke of him with affection and admiration as one fascinated by pebbles and thrilled by the winds and clouds. A pity, they wrote, that he never brought it all together, that such a clever, scholarly man never amounted to anything. The Jesuits in my day were very conscious of Hopkins, for whose poetry I had personally little taste until I was close to thirty. I was frightened by him. But I inherited from him one great blessing. The English Jesuits were determined never to be accused again of maltreating poets, so from quite early on I was handled with extreme, rather nervous and edgy liberality; not that I thought so at the time.

What can you learn about Britain in a place as islanded from history as the Jesuit noviceship was? We were often sent out walking all day, with a few coppers or no money at all. I therefore know or once knew the whole of west London and its approaches, and every reach of the Thames as far upstream as Maidenhead, and the old twopenny tram route from Wandsworth Hill to Lambeth Palace, every square inch of Westminster Abbey, every grove and corner of Bushey, Isleworth, Kew, Wimbledon, Barnes, Richmond, having explored it all on foot. The Roman camp on Wimbledon Common did not seem so bizarre to me then as it does today. But the river

Thames itself was what I loved; I dreamed of one day exploring its upper streams in Gloucestershire much as one might dream of going to Tibet. Now London, and the Thames in London, have altered so much in my lifetime, that I feel like a ghost from another and a more innocent and serious world. Runnymead, the Meads as we called it as schoolboys, used to be a perfectly empty place, utterly unfrequented and unknown, until people began to leave London at night during the Blitz, and camp in the nearest green desert. Now Runnymead is full of monuments and without meaning.

We learnt most as novices by talking to each other, most of all of course as youngsters from the older men. I made a friend then from the potteries whose family had scrabbled on spoil heaps for their winter fuel, and one from Glasgow whose stories of the Gorbals set my hair on end. Sawn-off shotguns fired through letter boxes were new to me. Someone in the merchant navy recalled his initiation into boiler-scraping at midsummer in the Red Sea. A shell-shocked artillery officer told me strange stories I have never forgotten about war and what it was like; he was only a few years older than I was. All his boyhood he had a recurring dream about finding a certain safe place in a desert. It came true when he was eighteen, in charge of a mobile gun, 'swanning about in the blue', as he put it. Even meeting boys from other schools, particularly Protestant ones like Shrewsbury and Taunton, was a new experience to me. Almost everyone seemed infinitely more mature than I was, and so I suppose they ought to have been. How odd it is to think that one will never again be so close to anyone, except one's innermost family, as one was to Jesuits around one's own age before one was twenty. The intimacy diminished over the years, but at the worst a quizzical friendship, sometimes a deep affection, takes its place.

We went out from Roehampton on Sunday mornings to teach religion in Sunday schools. Mine was in the Harrow Road, as rough a parish in as rough an area as you could well hope to find. The parish priest was Irish; he preached long sermons of furious denunciation, mostly directed against those who were absent from church. Afterwards we held our sessions in a subdivided, unheated cellar, darker and far grimier than the catacombs. The children were poor and distinctly ragged. The big change in dress, cleanliness and income that produced Mods versus Rockers by the end of the decade had hardly started in 1950. It was difficult to hold the children's attention. Some of us favoured 'visual aids', holy toys of various kinds, but those never lasted long enough. One was driven back on primitive story-telling, and if the lives of the saints were unexciting, one could always put in a pirate ship or some crocodiles to cheer them up.

The truth is that I at least was terrified of my pupils; they lived in a world I had never known. It was a long time before I learned. It is no use loving people unless you like them and they amuse you; it is a presumption, an impertinence. That is truest of all in a school. In my last year at Beaumont a history master called Mr Bond, a natural born antiquary and archivist who left to become Clerk of the Records to the House of Lords, had drawn a very broad-based triangle on a blackboard, to demonstrate what a tiny, privileged minority we belonged to. It took me many years to get to know the base of that triangle. The differences were extraordinary, unimagined. Down to 1945 a fourteen-year-old public schoolboy was by average a stone heavier than a fourteen-year-old at a state school. They say wartime rationing evened out all that, but it seems much more likely to be modern medical care for babies and small children.

However these things may be, there was also no doubt about the existence of clerical snobbery, which I observed at close range for many years. In our generation it began to wither away, probably because as novices we were so mixed. In the past the clergy, and the Jesuits more than most, had come from just a few schools. They were more uniform, and far more inbred and prejudiced. They belonged to my mother's world and not my father's. But it would not have occurred to us in 1950 that any work was demeaning or any company low. All the same, more than one young Jesuit in my day had terrible trouble because of an interest in social justice, or in those questions where the writings of the Popes have relevance to British economic and social problems. Even I, who was no fire-eater about such matters, was laughed out of court when I once asked to spend just a month or two working in the Cowley motor industry, only for the experience. It would be fair to say that throughout my training as a Jesuit, a clash of generations was taking place which has ended without my noticing it, only rather recently.

Once the first two years were over we took vows; from that moment we were Jesuits. Most of my friends had to do an academic year afterwards which was like going back to school, to brush up their school subjects and undergo a process like decompression after the intense noviceship: to make their compromises gently, and find a way of life they could live for a long time. But two of us were lucky enough to escape. Because we were due to read classics at Oxford, which is a four-year not a three-year degree, we were taken out of the ranks at once and promoted by a year. As they told us at the time, these things work out even in the end. We went straight off to begin philosophy, another three-year course, at a house called Heythrop, a huge baroque shell in the middle of empty, rain-smitten countryside.

CHAPTER FOUR

Nature's Priest

> The youth who daily further from the east
> Must travel still is Nature's priest.
>
> Wordsworth

HEYTHROP LOOMED in a dusk that was full of rooks. It looked dark and implacably formal, with later buildings sprawling round it. Its aspect as we saw it for the first time was that of a gigantic abandoned railway-station in the middle of a field. It was built by Archer for a Duke of Shrewsbury in the 1700s, then gutted by fire, subtly destroyed by heavy restoration, then abandoned, then restored again in even worse taste. Since that day in September of 1950, the house's last charm has been annihilated by still more appalling additions and conversions; yet it had great charm as I knew it once: great charm and a little grandeur.

There was nothing to do there, officially speaking, except read a limited repertory of books about Neo-Thomism and medieval Latin scholastic writers. You kept bees or you played football, or you made elderflower wine or repaired bicycles or walked foxhound puppies, or you built a secret wireless inside a book, much as the mood took you. As pupils we were treated like children and fed with teaspoons of bread and milk. But the system of learning into which we now entered was so remarkably odd that we spent most of our time examining that. Intellectually it was disastrous, not in the hectic and voguish way of a really debauching subject, but in a dry, stupefying, pedantic way. We ended our three years of philosophy knowing all the answers and considering none of the questions. What we were taught was mostly not untrue, compared to other philosophy, but it was common sense under tension stretched out into excruciating tedium.

Like boys at school, we learnt more from watching our mad professors than we did from the syllabus: a long, dry, thin man like a preserved banana, a melancholy, deep-thinking, musician, or a pink-cheeked Victorian ex-chemist like a demure old lady. Or an ex-chaplain from the Air Force, disgraced for a cover picture in *Picture Post* that showed him helping a WAAF with her make-up; he was still unashamed and grinning, he cut his own hair *en brosse* and had a long past of sensational failures. He was a refreshing mixture of devotion and impiety. When he was called in the morning, he put out the light at once with his toe. In the middle of Mass, which he said of course in Latin, he used to stop and exclaim about Latin usage, not out of anger but out of curiosity. '*Omnigenum. Omnigenum*? Funny use. *Omnigenum*. Hmm.' He taught me Greek, and I loved him, though I learnt little. My private spiritual adviser that year was another interrupter of his own Masses, with cries like 'Oh God, where is it? Oh God, why *did* you make me such a *bloody* fool?' He was always trying to become a monk, but without success. His life's work, unless it was the crazy comfort he gave people like me, was a huge unpublished typescript about the archaeology of the Roman catacombs. He had a sharp nose and gleaming glasses, like a comic nun, like a comic Cardinal Newman.

These were by no means the most eccentric characters in that great stranded ark. Age and the wind and the alcohol of books would drive anyone mad who stayed there long enough. The theological library, which being officially too young to use I had to enter by a bathroom window and a scramble over the roof, smelt intoxicating, but large parts of it were terribly unread. The standard commentary on the Acts of the Apostles had uncut pages from 1912 until I cut them in 1962. But those were not the treasures I was really after. My bottled-up curiosity had matured by now into a bad attack of 'hydroptic thirst for knowledge', and I was also hungry for literature, a slightly different thing. Of the books in that labyrinthine attic library, I recall best the first editions of the sermons of John Donne, and an early edition, perhaps the first, of Wordsworth's *Prelude*.

Other avenues being blocked, my real life was mostly in the woods. Heythrop itself was charming but the grounds were thrilling. You heard sheep and lambs in the day and foxes barking at night. The calling of the plovers and the cawing of rooks were ordinary voices. Then a weedy, swimmable chain of lakes, Victorian woods and secret copses, violets and cowslips and orchids and autumn crocuses, and the great avenue of lime trees, every one a rookery, would have attracted anyone. They invited us into a freedom we had forgotten for two years. The loneliest and dullest of tramps through the soaking lanes was exhilarating at that time as the most picturesque of newly-discovered places in childhood. But the grounds of Heythrop had been planted or replanted in Victorian times; they were all nooks and crannies and solitary twisting paths. Their masterpiece was a great amphitheatre of rockeries above a round pond with an island, with the skeleton of an Iceland whale hanging from iron hooks in a hidden grotto in the rocks, and a gentle water-spring.

Long walks were encouraged. In spring and autumn the weather was gentle, though I remember storms in summer and muggy wet days. Heythrop was just at the beginning of the Cotswolds, on the first serious swelling, high enough above sea-level and the Oxford plain to get some heavy doses of snow in winter but not high enough for that pure air that blows about the higher hilltops above Broadway and Birdlip. The easiest walks took us across country to the Evenlode valley and the last remains of Wichwood. Elm trees stood in every hedge. The circle of everyday walking distance included Blenheim lakes, the stone circle at Rollright, and the standing stones of prehistoric graves around it, and the mysterious, lovely village of Great Tew with apricot trees on every cottage, a valley where sheep were still driving out people in the middle of this century. But the more adventurous you were, the further you got. On some days, or was it only for some excuses, we had bicycles.

We lived in the country all right, but without living in a village, and without that sense and presence of a village that even the grandest private houses have. We pumped our own water and generated our own electricity. The ugly and comforting noise of rams and generators speaks about peace in my recollection much as an old threshing machine or combine harvester does to others. There was a ram I used to pass sometimes at night; that ram, and a vixen barking near what were called the Gas Cottages, whose only light was oil-lamps, and the steady chewing noise of cattle in the ground-mist, almost abolish thirty years, and I can feel the wetness again soaking through my shoes, I can smell the mist and see that night's piece of moon and a few stars. How old were the field names, I wonder? How old was the name Foxbury Wood? It was an entangled place with some very old trees, felled now most of them; you could smell the foxes in the river-bottom, a penetrating, unmistakable smell like rotten cabbage.

Heythrop must have been nothing but rough grass and bits of woods until it was enclosed to make an estate. Most of it was poor land, and where the London to Stratford road ran alongside it on Broadstone Hill, it used to be favoured by highwaymen. Conditions in all that countryside were so primitive even within my memory that where the old pub called The Quiet Woman used to stand, with three or four cottages round it on the main road, the only water came from one pump, and there was one man who used to take a bath under it every morning stark naked by the roadside. Cottages where you could see the stars through the roof were not uncommon before the war. Nor was rent at half a crown. The settlement of North Oxfordshire villages had not altered much since the Middle Ages. The names on the oldest gravestones were the ones you still heard in the village hall. In English villages until yesterday, historians tell us that the poorer you were, the closer to home you married. Many a village had its special disease developed over centuries of inbreeding.

Wichwood Forest sends more than its ration of simple or half-witted people to Littlemore mental hospital. At Hook Norton the people used to have wens on their necks and the hens could swim. I complimented a young lad once in Hook Norton on how polite they all were to their elders. 'Ah yes,' he said, 'that's because in this village no one knows who his father is, so we has to be polite to 'em all.' The last new blood that entered Hook Norton until very recent times must have come with the workmen who made the railway, a fine place for badgers now where no train will ever run again. Nor does anyone today conceive how isolated small villages used to be.

A hundred years or so ago, before the Victorians built a church and a school at Leafield, the people of Leafield had nowhere to bury their dead. So a party of them carried a coffin down through the forest, across Cornbury Park woods to Charlbury. They happened to see a squirrel, so they let their friend rest while they organized a squirrel hunt. Then it came on to snow, and it snowed thicker and thicker, and then the snow lay for weeks. They never could find that coffin again until the snow thawed, though they say it came to no harm. That story comes from a man whose grandfather remembered it.

The more isolated a village is, the more admirably ungovernable its people are, the more themselves. It may be that the old underlying map of tribal England, which in its cruder boundaries you can still feel today, has not been eroded by time, but intensified. Those mysterious boundaries that marketing surveys discover between preferences for different food or drink still correspond to the tribal divisions of Britain: so do the regions of each traditional way of cooking. So does the style of countryside and architecture. But few people realize how intensely the underlying difference of blood and culture used to be felt.

It survives as jokes. They still tell you in Hook Norton about a fire in Chipping Norton where the Hook Norton fire-engine got there first. In Stonesfield they still call the next village 'silly Combe where they put the pig on the wall to watch the band go by'. No one knows why. And they raise their eyebrows at Finstock and all the forest villages. Years ago we used to believe the Wichwood people had a distinct physical, racial type. Now that I live under the edge of the forest I can no longer maintain that; I no longer see the wood for the trees perhaps. At the Domesday survey the whole forest had I think fourteen recorded families. No doubt there were others in the woods. This was once the refuge of Wicci, a tribe that Bede records. I am not disinclined to think that those are the people you meet on the Witney bus.

Some stories are too wild to credit: they belong to folklore, though they must have an explanation of some kind. The usual story told of the Rollright Stones is that once a year on All Souls Night, or New Year's Night, or when midnight strikes in Long Compton, they run down to the brook to drink. They were an army turned to stone, and the King of them is the tall stone standing alone with one foot in Warwickshire. The group of five are the Whispering Knights. The King was moving north when he met a witch up on the Rollright ridge, and she said this:

> Seven long strides shalt thou take:
> If long Compton thou canst see,
> King of England shalt thou be.

The point of the story so far is that the Rollright stones are just out of sight of Long Compton. That village lies below the swelling of the hill, safely out of sight.

But one day they say the stones will come to life and the King will reign. We must assume that means the end of Long Compton. As it is, when the stones run downhill to drink, any human being in their way is said to get crushed to death. Two men really were killed when a farmer took down a stone. They say two horses had trouble dragging it downhill; it fell and killed the two labourers, and then one horse drew it uphill easily. Other stones not far away are said to go drinking at night: the Hoar Stone at Enstone and the Hawk Stone at Spelsbury. What the witch said to the King as he drew near to Warwickshire was this:

Long Compton thou carsn't see,
King of England thou shalt not be.
Rise, stick, and stand stone:
King of England thou shalt be none.
Thou and thy men hoar-stones shall be
and I myself an eldern tree.

The King and his army became the Rollright Stones, and the witch or her stick became a tree. At midsummer, when that tree blossomed, people not long ago used to come up from Long Compton; when the tree was cut they say the Kingstone nodded his head. We know also that in 1742 and in the nineteenth century 'people from Wales', surely the drovers, chipped away small pieces from that stone, 'to keep the Devil off'. So far we are still in the area of folklore, where beautiful and ridiculous elements mingle and meaning almost dies out; people do not know really what they are doing, there is no secret wisdom. But we can add something.

This is a Long Compton story, not a Rollright story: people climbed the hill to the stones, and the stones went downhill to drink. It is also true, or certainly was so in the fifties and sixties, that Long Compton had a bad reputation in other villages for witchcraft and magic, not without actual scandal in the graveyard, caused by outsiders surely. But since the war, or so I was told as a very young man by an old clergyman, there have been at least two murders in the circle of the Rollright stones, both without solution, apparently unmotivated. However that may be, it is certain that on the right night of the year people still do climb the hill in the darkness, and if outsiders are waiting to see what happens, then they simply sit down and freeze them out.

In my first years at Heythrop I felt I could understand England better by knowing such stories. All the same, it was the reality of the countryside that obsessed me more than its prehistory. What I went to Rollright to feel was the texture of the lichen on the stones and the softness of the grass. We ate blackberries from the hedge and fried field-mushrooms. I spent my twenty-first birthday lying in the grass by the river Evenlode, beside a wood full of orchids and calling cuckoos. But even without wanting to, I began to get a strong sense of boundaries, both in time and in history. Villages like Stonesfield, Stunsfield or Stuntasfield, which means fool's field, being full of stones more valuable than grazing ground I suppose, so that the fool was justified, and Charlbury, the burgh of Ceorl's people, and Spelsbury, the look-out place (what did it look at if not the forest?) convey the atmosphere of the Anglo-Saxon countryside rather well. Ditchley is the Devil's ditches, which are still to be seen. Enstone is Enna's stone, maybe the Hoar Stone on the edge of the village; Tew means the ridge, and Woodstock is just a place in the woods.

The late Roman British, the people whose hero Arthur was, were mysterious to me. I was coming to hate the later Middle Ages and value a Britain the Normans had crushed into the grass. Perhaps like grass it sprang up again, as I still believe. Most of what we are supposed to admire in the Middle Ages was a classical survival or an oriental import. Even the Bible was written in Hebrew and Greek. The cloister is only a forum. The tall architecture of abbeys comes from re-using classical columns or imitating those who did so. The famous Norman details and early Romanesque carvings, which are all over Oxfordshire, are obvious Anglo-Saxon work. The Normans were only interested in castles and heavy metal, so it seemed to me. At that time I found Langland a more stirring poet than Chaucer, in his language and his metre and his social views. As for the land around me, I was content to be drunk 'where seven drunken Englands lie buried one in one'.

It was about now that I came to drown myself in the poetry of David Jones. Many things in my life, and particularly in this book, look by hindsight like weak echoes of his poetry, but I do not think the influence was direct. He was not only a writer and painter of Blake-like greatness and originality, but in the course of time he became one of my most loved friends. In a way it was chance that gave us so many interests in common, Roman Britain, human prehistory, the 1914 war, and the whole unfolding of modern art and literature, as well as tastes and distastes. He sat in a bedsitting room in Harrow like an angel designed by Leonardo da Vinci to work mechanically, or a sympathetic hermit conceived by Edward Lear. He was one of very few really great artists I have ever known. In December 1974 I preached his funeral sermon[1]. He has always been a powerful underground influence in my life.

David is the poet of a continuity which I was learning slowly by physical experience. Nothing could convey this physical sensation of continuity better than an excavation which I attended by chance in the summer when I was twenty. We were recruited as a labour-force to dig a Roman house that lay lightly buried under a Dutch barn and a yard, at Beaconsfield Farm, Great Tew. The smell of straw and the sunshine and the little boys running up and down, the real, slow-seeming life of the farm going on around us, and the reappearance of the old floors, the piles of painted plaster and the thick lintel of puddled limestone which was so hard to break through, then add the cycle ride with a bag of sandwiches in the early morning, and home at night through stony villages; it all composed one harmonious world. In the ruins of the Roman heating system, which had been disturbed before, we found eighteenth-century wine-glasses and a pair of spectacles. A foot or two under the surface trodden by cattle and rutted by

[1] *Requiem Sermon for David Jones*, see Appendix

tractors, we came on the skeleton of a Saxon with an eighth-century knife in his back. He seemed to lie as he must have fallen. The coroner came to no conclusion.

A little later all that mass of painted plaster, which I believe was then the most ever recorded from a single Roman house in this country, was packed into crates and lost by British Rail. I was shocked at the time, and the disappointment to the youthful excavators must have been hard for them to bear, but it now pleases me in a way. I am glad the Roman farmhouse has gone back to ground under Beaconsfield Farm. I am glad it has gone native. It fills me with an odd pride that I was the first and last person in more than a thousand years to scrub the mosaic floor, which was in good Victorian taste, of someone's Roman farm buildings at Great Tew. It led to nothing: even in my own life it had no result really for another ten years. But experience gives one the feel of things. It was an initiation, although in memory so long afterwards it recalls nothing about the Romans, only the smell of straw in that farmyard, the taste of sandwiches, and the shadows of the trees as we bicycled home.

After philosophy was put to bed, we moved forward to be trained as teachers in London. My first teaching assignment was a long way down the Old Kent Road, at the Mawbey Road secondary modern school. I learnt a great deal about London and a little about teaching, but I doubt if the pupils learnt much. The school was a small, depressing institution, housed on the upper floor of a hideous late-Victorian building which the bombs had rattled but not destroyed. It was decorated indoors with special Government paint like adhesive pea-soup. The lower floors belonged to the Educationally Subnormal, referred to only as ESN for fear their feelings might be hurt. Our floor were a lively lot; the gloomy old Scotsman who taught scientific drawing was chased up the Old Kent Road by a gang of them armed with bicycle chains. This boisterous prank was only meant to tease him. One thing worked on the senior boys like magic; it always produced perfect peace and quiet for as much as two hours. Half way through the afternoon, when the oldest teacher was fed up with teaching, he had only to lean back and say 'Get out your paints boys.' The snakes slept on the heads of the furies. The classroom remained as tranquil as the quietest nursery until the bell ended the day.

By coincidence, or else because of a boredom and longing that rivalled the feelings of my pupils, it was during those two years that I began to be passionate about English watercolour paintings, and to discover through them a freshness that decorated the hoariest antiquity. In those days one could still have bought a Cotman or a David Cox for ten pounds. But I no more thought of possessing pictures than of buying the landscape itself. Those artists were masters of the soul and the eye and the place, they taught you how to see, just because they never spoke. Was there such a crispness really in the air, in Norfolk or in Northumberland two hundred years ago? Did I really see for myself the yellow and the green leaves yesterday in a pool of light, or had Cotman taught me speechlessly to see them? I put myself to school to these very English artists until the word topographic meant more to me than other words. Painters like Cotman never cease to be surprising, their teaching is inexhaustible, they give the freshest pleasure. They sharpened my appetite for places, landscape, antiquities, until it became an intense hunger.

I have the impression now that many of us were old-fashioned in the early fifties. My idols in poetry after Shakespeare were not Auden or Pound in 1954, but Spenser (the minor poems) and Ronsard and Dante (the more obvious bits). In those two years I read my way through Burckhardt on the Italian Renaissance in the bath; it took a year and a half of soaking. I also consumed dialogues of Plato like hot toast and butter. My favourite painters on the grand scale were Rembrandt, Stubbs and Watteau, and I must admit to my shame that I still secretly preferred Rex Whistler's murals in the tea rooms of the Tate Gallery to most of what one saw upstairs. There is no excuse for any of this; the one advantage of my unprogressiveness was that a slow, leisurely development from being backward and provincial to thinking the same as everyone else is educative in its way. The particular world that I and my like still thought of as modern and promising was really an old, dying world. I went one evening after school to Evensong in the Abbey, to see Vaughan Williams lay a wreath on the grave of Stanford. It was a dark night in early winter, the cold and the dead leaves and darkness seemed to have got inside the Abbey. The Dean read in his stall by a desk lamp from Revelations. 'And there came forth from the throne thunderings and lightenings and mutterings.' Old Vaughan Williams shuffled up the aisle almost alone, in carpet slippers, nodding his old head like an owl; he was holding an enormous circular wreath of pink roses.

CHAPTER FIVE

A Silver Poker

> There was a supply of waiters from the colleges who would come in. The grandest was Mr Moon who carried a silver poker before University processions.
>
> Carola Oman, *An Oxford Childhood*

IT WAS AT OXFORD that everything altered for me. I went there in 1954, to read classics. Campion Hall was where young Jesuits studied secular subjects. They lived under discipline, but they were farmed out to more or less normal tutors. We were housed in a smart, grim parody of an ecclesiastical building, designed by Lutyens and created or conjured like a rabbit out of a top hat by Father D'Arcy, who had left it to its own devices long ago. It stood in an obscure lane that ran outside the Oxford city wall, in the town ditch, not far from Pembroke and Christ Church. At that time we had a long, old-fashioned garden with a very old pear tree and a horse chestnut tree. That was an oasis of stillness. We ventured out, timidly at first, into the city and the university. We were scholarly and shy and very anxious to live up to the grand expectations which Martin D'Arcy had dropped on our heads like a conjurer's magic mantle. But as time went on we found our level, and for some of us the world sprang open like an oyster.

In the winter my chief pleasure was beagling. Once a week a bus left the Canterbury Gate of Christ Church for Adderbury or Denchworth or Garsington or Waterperry. We wandered in the fields, stubble fields with heartsease and blue speedwell flourishing here and there between the furrows, or over flooded pastures with snow-patches, or through deep green river-meadows under the bare, luminous downs. The hounds streamed away, rooks cawed, hares ran or hid. Often enough not a hare was caught, but that was no worry to me, because I always went beagling with the same friend and we were deep in conversation. That conversation lasted with a few interruptions for many years. We trotted or ambled together across the countryside, and stood to gaze as the yellow or pink stains of winter sunset drained out of the sky. The falling sun flamed in a hundred reflections from the windows of lonely houses, or it gleamed in the dark pools under our feet. The Berkshire Downs took on a pale, ghostly colour that was hardly green; the sky was hardly blue. Sometimes the sky was full of larks. One late afternoon the hounds outdistanced everybody. We saw them running dead straight on the track of a fox. As they vanished into a wood, two or three roe deer, a fox and five or six young hares came racing out in the opposite direction.

What did we talk about? Anything and everything: a lot of history. My friend was a medieval historian called Denis Bethell, enchanting, humorous, kindly, and brave. He had huge spectacles and no money to speak of, but I have never met anyone with more cheerfulness or a greater or more sustained intellectual curiosity. His range was magnificent, and his gleeful dedication to scholarly research was obviously an essential part of his personality. We shared many enthusiasms, some of which no doubt I learnt from Denis. I took him to Sir John Beazley's lectures on Greek vase-painting and Fraenkel's on Catullus; he took me to the Archaeology Society and Professor Hoskins on the history of the English landscape. In summer we punted up rivers, streams, canals, every backwater and every wet ditch. Summer or winter, we walked more miles a week than I now walk in half a year. In or around Oxford we left no ancient stone unturned. We knew the places Matthew Arnold knew, and others of our own. At the end of Trinity terms we walked to London, through the night. We used to have dinner first in college or in some small, upstairs restaurant where in those days you could get a Spanish omelette and half a bottle of wine each and have change from a pound. As the shadows deepened and the roads cleared, we set out. There was a lorry-drivers' halt on the way that served bacon sandwiches until midnight. Sometimes we took a fancy route, through Ewelme or by way of the beech woods behind Nettlebed, by Stonor into Henley. Usually we followed the main London road over the Chilterns by High Wycombe. Term ended about Midsummer Eve, so that was the night we walked. The sky scarcely grew dark until it was nearly light again. The last rose colours of sunset were still in the west when the beech woods swallowed us up as we climbed the Chilterns somewhere near Chinnor; by the time we got clear of the trees, and out onto the top of the hill, dawn was in the east. The night was cool and dewy; for three or four hours no traffic moved. The Chiltern beech woods were like Uccello's *Hunt in the Forest*, and the dawn chorus, just above West Wycombe, was the loudest noise one had ever heard. It was thousands of birds.

I recollect one year Denis and me washing in the Thames at Henley, having left Paul Cooper asleep in a haystack. Where is he now? Last heard of as an archaeologist and a historian of the Roman army. He kept an academic lodging house in Rome for mildly Bohemian scholars. One night they brought in some film people celebrating the end of a film, and the next morning Paul found a live lion left in his kitchen. Another year of walking, I recollect only a spectacular breakfast in a grand hotel. Walking at night suited us. The only disturbance was occasionally being stopped by the police. Once we were asked had we stolen a motorbike. Why would we be tramping along with walking sticks if we had a motorbike? 'Ah that might just be your cleverness Sir, mightn't it?' We never got right into London. We parted after breakfast and took a suburban bus or train.

Although the opening of the eyes I experienced through

Denis was not really a matter of seeing places, since he travelled far more than I did in England and Wales at that time, yet I suppose that little by little, through long walks from Oxford, one for example through Hampshire to see Gilbert White's Selborne, and one into Kent to the freakish monastery of Aylesford, and then through cycling overnight to Wales and a long series of North Wales holidays, and through otter-hunting in rivers all over Devonshire and the Welsh marches, I did at last get some grip on the bones of southern Britain. Britannia's shield and lower half, but not quite the tip of her trident. I am not willing to defend the hunting of so many hares, and even less so the otters, though I never saw more than one otter killed, and that was a saddening night. I doubt if I would hunt anything today, but I will not pretend to regret my memories utterly. I am very glad to have seen hounds at work, and they took me into many beautiful rivers and pools, often up to my neck. The hounds delighted us both, so did the tinny horn. Countryside reveals itself to those who follow hounds on foot with an intimacy and a dash of excitement which I count among the greatest benefits of good luck in my life. Horsey people and hunting people seem to many of my friends painfully conventional. To me, that not being my world when the chips are down, they seem exotic and amusing. I suppose the only quite innocent form of hunting I have ever done was following foxes alone on foot by smell, but for that one needs a friend with a good nose.

What I learnt mostly from Denis was bound to be history. He taught me to revere the ruins of monasteries; the long poem *Ruined Abbeys*, which I wrote a few years later as a film script, owes everything to him. He got me over resenting the Middle Ages, and made me love the limestone skeletons of that vanished life.

> Here death was never quite at home,
> in fields not chosen for dying
> they simply slept and lie sleeping
> and shall lie till the crack of doom.

And I hope to be one who dies
with simple ruins in his eyes.

Selden says somewhere that antiquaries have no fear of death left, because their whole study and life's occupation has to do with it; they have come to love death. I am sure that is true. Denis spent the last afternoon of his life listening to *Pickwick Papers* and roaring with laughter. As for Selden, he was one of our minor heroes; for some reason we had read his notes to Drayton's *Poly-Olbion*, and we liked anyone remotely connected with Izaak Walton. I have sometimes hoped to find a pair of Selden's spectacles, which he used to lose in profusion by marking his place with them in his books. One often finds Selden's copy of a book in the Bodleian, but librarians have had the spectacles out of them long ago. Denis having been brought up in the Church of England forced me, whether he wished it or not, to see what I can only call Anglican England, which had been quite invisible to me before, and without which there is no understanding our history even in the Middle Ages. Of course one needs to see a Catholic England as well, a much more bizarre attempt for most people. One needs both. At the very end of my training as a Jesuit, these things came together for me when I read as a practical guide to life the three tall volumes of David Knowles' *Monastic Order in England*, one of Denis's favourite books.

The most hungrily awaited moment of our usual week in Oxford was a straggling class which would nowadays be labelled a seminar, a long table of those interested, in a long room with motorcycle engines brooming at the traffic lights outside. This session was held by Dr Richard Hunt, Keeper of the Western manuscripts, a man so loved he was father-figure to half the scholars of Europe. His title resounded like Count of the Saxon Shore, the defender of ancient civilization in this island in the late Roman Empire. In his learning and generosity and in the antiquity of his bicycle he almost lived up to this analogy. He lectured in a small, high voice rather faint than fluting, with a slight stutter which he could use when he wanted, to dramatic effect. Some evenings one heard little but the broom-broom of the engines. His subject was the descent of manuscripts from one copy to another, from the ancient world to the Renaissance.

Nothing could have been more interesting to Denis and me, and no one could have been more learned about it than he was. But every year he began at the beginning, and by the end of his course we never got far beyond the ninth century, only occasionally raising our eyes to the hills to discuss the revival of green ink in the twelfth. He could tell by stroking a manuscript where the goat or sheep came from that was slaughtered to make it. Under his arm as he entered might be such an unregarded item as the manuscript of Pliny that King John used to take out hunting with him. That manuscript had a marginal note saying 'Notice this marvel about a dolphin, where a boy swims on a dolphin's back.' Then one October, to everyone's excitement, Dr Hunt decided to begin at the end and work backwards. He started with a flourish from the Renaissance itself, and every year thereafter for some time he did the same, but alas there was always a dark place in the middle Middle Ages that he never reached, either backwards or forwards.

The Renaissance was a game that everyone played. A classicist was in the strong position of knowing the things that later cultures were supposed to have rediscovered. There were those who spoke of a French, even of an English Renaissance, but these are bastard shadows of the moon. I was securely anchored to Burckhardt's description of what the Renaissance really was. It took place in Italy, and it consisted of the recovery of the classics and of quite particular social and political and cultural conditions, and the transformation of Byzantine painting, and a secular spirit like a groan of the forest wind, a blast of the Alpine wind; also of private pretensions, dreams, philsophies. The cleverer you were, the further back you pushed the Renaissance in Italy, until it almost met the diminishing influence of the antique world. What used to be called the Dark Ages was in my day just beginning to be called the late Roman Empire. All kinds of early flashes in the dark were being called the Renaissance.

> Why do the shepherds shout 'Ut Hoy!'
> And the lambs dance?
> It is an intellectual joy,
> The Renaissance.

Denis and I had our Renaissance back in the twelfth century; we had our eye on the tenth, and on Byzantium. That was when under his guidance I began to probe into the intense images, the moving history, and the cloudy achievements of the Anglo-Saxons. But we lived in an intellectually mixed world, as all young people do. Picasso and Braque and I think Matisse were alive; we admired them beyond measure. But Sir Maurice Bowra, who lent a friend of ours the latest and most expensive publication of Picasso's newest drawings, gave a great party in Oxford for Robert Frost, and I have seldom been more excited to meet anyone, because Frost knew Edward Thomas. Edward Thomas and Picasso were physically contemporaries, after all, although they were worlds apart in their spirit.

We fell head over heels into modern poetry as if it was a duckpond. We fumbled away at Anglo-Saxon Latin manuscripts, while we most deeply loved the Renaissance, and learnt from Constantine Tryphanis, the Professor of Medieval Greek and our only grown-up friend in those days, about the decadence and the fall of Byzantium. The first time in my life that I ever went abroad, in the early spring of 1956, was to Venice and to Florence. In Venice one stepped out of Mussolini's railway-station straight into a painting by Guardi, and so one still does. At Florence the aged aristocracy were still complaining about the ugly apparatus of the trams. Most people left Florence, I was told by an ancient lady, when the trams came. We lived on a hill in the Villa Machiavelli, and rambled about in solitary groves. We visited I Tatti only to see

Berenson's anemones, which I recollect as disappointing. His garden was not dry enough. The biggest thrill apart from Fra Angelico's convent and the Duomo itself, which haunts one everywhere, splendidly looming above narrow streets, and apart from Botticelli's *Spring*, and the *Birth of Venus*, anyway the greatest secret thrill, was the *Codex Amiatinus*.

Dr Hunt had talked about this eminent manuscript. When the monastery, or Christian learned institute, of Cassiodorus, south of Rome, was sold up in the seventh century, a passing Anglo-Saxon saint called Benet Biscop bought its Bible. One ought not to be surprised at a learned Northumbrian. Cassiodorus himself had been secretary and historian to the King of the Goths. His scholarly monastery was the fruit of his old age. The Bible journeyed on muleback across the Alps to be copied twice in Northumberland. One of these copies, with an Anglo-Saxon inscription on its flyleaf, survived the Middle Ages peacefully in an obscure mountain monastery in North Italy; it is called the *Codex Amiatinus*. The other survived in Durham Chapter library, where a generation ago one could actually hear the champing and crunching of the bookworms in the parchment. Odd pages of that copy have turned up as wrapping round packages of eighteenth-century letters in a nobleman's attic, and more recently as lampshades in the Durham antique shops. The *Codex Amiatinus* has some importance for the textual history of the New Testament in Latin. It seemed to symbolize all I most valued in the history of Europe in the Dark Ages: the scraping together of antique remnants, the hoarding of scholarly knowledge, the Anglo-Saxon missionaries setting out to christianize their persecutors, the Latin New Testament itself. I was determined to see the library where I supposed it might be on exhibition.

I presented myself at the Laurentian library in Florence with what little Italian I could weave into a piece. They asked me for a letter of introduction or a card. I produced my Oxford certificate of matriculation, which being in Latin got me past the guard at the outside door. I had by heart a sentence meaning I have come from a vast distance solely to see certain manuscripts, and behold, the museum is closed; is it by your kindness permitted to see the directress? Eventually I made it into the presence of this kind but puzzled lady. What were these manuscripts that I so desired to see? For a start, I said, the *Codex Amiatinus*. She sat me down in the reading room, and they brought it. It took two men to carry, and eight volumes of an encyclopedia to prop up. I did not dare move from it all day, and I think that was only volume one. I had somehow supposed my *Codex* was a slim, pretty New Testament. It was a gigantic Bible of awe-inspiring beauty and rigorous plainness. Of all the mistakes I could have made, that one was the most rewarding. As dusk fell, I crept away, having had a long read of the Bible in Latin.

One of the recurring features of Anglo-Saxon life was that not only bishops but kings thrust into exile or at the end of their natural lives often went to Rome, to the graves of the apostles. The place where they lived in Rome was called until recently the Borgo, the Burgh, and its name still lingers in the street name, Borgo Santo Spirito, which always used to strike me with a chill of fear, being the address of the Jesuit headquarters, a source of unpredictable calamities. These small burghs or boroughs, the armed encampments of Franks and Lombards and Frisians, all but surrounded the Vatican in the early Middle Ages. They were independent for civil and also military purposes; in effect they were tiny independent states or settlements as the Vatican is today. That makes it, for me at least, somehow easier to swallow the proclamation of Latin and Greek and Hebrew writings in a thirteenth-century or even a much earlier building in the empty centre of a North Oxfordshire village every Sunday of the year.

Denis and I did not think of ourselves as backward-looking in our interests, or oddly specialized; nor were we. One explores at that age in every direction at once. If it is true that there are no explanations except historical explanations, then one is bound to look into many corners of history at one time.

When a friend of ours wrote in a poem some years later of a career scholar, 'browsing among manuscripts, like a pensioned-off racehorse', that appeared to me as a very funny description of my ideal life, though it was not true of Denis. I, being a Latinist or a Hellenist, had the excuse of believing that manuscripts and their history, if one only sat down and sorted them out, would hold the key to the lost, dusty poetry of the ancient world. In reality, a lot of work of this kind goes a very short way indeed, and it takes a lifetime to make serious inroads. The most important intellectual influence on me at that time, and by far the greatest teacher I have ever known, was Eduard Fraenkel, so it is curious that I never appreciated his constant maxim; that learning was easy, and all too common in Oxford, but what was needed was judgement. I was too overwhelmed by his learning to take that maxim in until too late.

Denis was a person of Johnsonian common sense, though one of his favourite, and our favourite quotations was a couplet by Richard Wilbur:

> Kick on, Sam Johnson, till you break your bones,
> But cloudy, cloudy, is the stuff of stones.

Maybe the most Johnsonian thing about Denis was his household in Monkstown, which resembled the Doctor's in the romantic generosity with which it was conducted, in its variety of inhabitants and the economic chaos of his arrangements. It is curious how rare in modern life the Bohemian scholar has become, although with money as tight as it is today, we may see more of them in future. Oxbridge dons are mostly too dull and prim, too professional and competent to be called Bohemian except in their most secret vices. Denis had a deep disturbance of soul that Samuel Johnson would have recognized. He actually loved his pupils; he actually loved his subject. He was temperamentally, although never actually, an alcoholic. He might perfectly easily have developed in twenty more years into an imaginative learned man of the calibre and fame of Tolkein or C. S. Lewis. I am not talking about their fiction but their conversation, their human authority, and their learned work.

You could never revisit any monument or gallery with Denis without seeing something freshly. Whether it was a fantastical piece of architectural detail in Broad Street, or the view from a roof in Longwall, some trees weeping into the Oxford canal, or the hundredth time of gazing at Dutch flower paintings or the *Hunt in the Wood*, he would always see something quite obvious I had never before noticed. He was a born noticer, a quality that no one can fake and which plays, as memory does, a very big part in all intelligence, and in scholarly imagination. No locked door in Oxford defeated us, except a collection of hundreds of musical boxes that played tunes of the 1800s, said to be stored in a cellar under the Natural History Museum. With Denis I explored the old canal basin and the offices of the Oxford Canal Company, then derelict, now underneath Nuffield College. We got the prison governor's permission to explore the lovely vault under Oxford Castle, and the well inside the green mound they used to use for hanging. We got the porter of the Mitre's help to explore the range of cellars under that, which extend far beyond the property. There are things and places I still see with his eyes.

One of them is Westminster Abbey. It must surely be thought, with the exception perhaps of the Lindisfarne Gospels and that great rain-soaked, stranded ship the Cathedral of Winchester, which always seems to me to have strayed up the Ichen from Southampton and petrified, that the Abbey is the greatest monument of early English Christianity. What impresses visitors at Durham is comparatively simple and a matter of situation. Early Christian sculpture in the Severn valley has an intoxicating wildness and strangeness, it gives an extraordinary effect of crisp and charming simplicity, it belongs to the marginal territory between two worlds. It belongs to Mercia, more exciting than Wessex. Nothing could be more fascinating. The Alfred jewel at Oxford has a delicacy and a strength, and a more than Byzantine intensity. But the complicated Abbey at Westminster, just because so many later elements have clustered into its fabric, appears clearly at once and to everyone to derive from its single, remote origin. At Westminster Wren looks almost like a medieval architect, and the eighteenth-century monuments and the royal tombs cling appropriately round the dusky skirts of Edward the Confessor. He is the whole point of the place.

It is a pity we are not allowed to take away the Rood screen, to reveal the Confessor's tomb as it was meant to be seen, high up and distant, down the whole length of the church. The Normans built it, and it was intended, like the Cathedral of Winchester with its shrine behind the altar and the Kings of Wessex buried all round it, to validate the coronation of Norman monarchs in England. As a piece of petrified propaganda, the Abbey does its work magnificently to this day. Only they ought to remove the rood screen, and take up the sanctuary carpet. I once had a part in a ceremony at Westminster, and during rehearsal I happened to stumble over the edge of the carpet and see what lay below it, a floor of dark and splendid mosaic that might have been made for Saint Mark's in Venice, and not very different in date from the floor of Saint Mark's. Of the colours I remember dark green porphyry, imperial purple and turquoise, and I think a yellow stone. That floor must I suppose be by the Cosmati brothers, who worked on the tomb itself. In feeling, it belongs to Anglo-Saxon rather than to Norman England.

It is very hard to forgive the Normans for their near suppression of the English language. Their bloodiness to the bones of English saints, which they subjected to ordeal by fire, is a comparatively small matter. Their murders and their massacres were dealt out impartially. But they destroyed a culture, a social organization, a forest of trees, and what had flowered in *Beowulf* and *The Seafarer*, a language that was the envy of Europe, fruited for hundreds of years after 1066 only in religious tales and carols. Perhaps things are not quite as simple as I am saying, because the whole history of our language is still stuck all over the literature like barnacles. Certain medieval English poems stretch backwards into a half-light, into paganism. Danish ballad refrains, and Viking superstitions and place names, speak as clearly as white hair and blue eyes do about the many hundreds of years when these islands looked like part of Scandinavia. That is what physically they are, after all. The Orkneys are as much border territory as the Channel Isles; or better, they are uninvaded solitudes, a place of their own, starlight above the crest of Britannia.

English when it revived was a language of resistance. Its first great works on any scale were the *Robin Hood* ballads, which missed becoming an epic only by a whisker, and that long, angry rumble of a poem, that never-ending summer thunderstorm, *Piers Plowman*. Of course Chaucer was also worth waiting for, and courtly and European as he is, his suppleness and the greatness of his sheer art bring his England to life in a way the angrier poems fail to do. There are those who maintain anyway that *Robin Hood* was just a fantasy for the middle classes. But *Robin Hood*'s likeness to medieval outlaw poems in other cultures of the same date away at the far end of Europe, in Serbo-Croat and in Greek, makes that unlikely.

So went these yeomen to the wood
as light as leaf on linden tree.

Almost nothing is quite without its consolation, and if Anglo-Saxon, English poetry, and with it a nation, a whole culture, came to an end in a generation, after 1066, at least the *Song of Roland*, one of the greatest of medieval poems, survives in its best form only in an English, not a French manuscript, in French with at least an Anglo-French colouring.

And yet how can it have taken so many beginnings stamped out, so many massacres and invasions, and the utter disappearance of languages and cultures, to produce the Britain we live in? This history is continuous, disastrous, endlessly repetitive. Neither God nor man can think it was worthwhile. The generations never born, the ancient British language lost, Welsh culture pitiably deprived and crushed, Irish Gaelic all but lost, Cornish evaporated, the British murdered and herded by Saxons, the Saxons by the Danes and Vikings, the English by the Normans, then the Irish and the Welsh suffering the same. The English learnt to treat inferiors from the way they treated one another and then the Irish; they practised that lesson on the American Indians, then on the Irish again, on slaves of every colour, and finally on the Scots, hounded after 1745 like wild animals, blasted from the sea, driven from the land and some transported into literal slavery in America.

I do not think my friend would have denied any of this, although it has taken me most of my life to grasp it. We were both as young men mildly enraged, Attlee-type socialists, though neither of us voted very often, and culturally we were natural conservatives, as many poets and historians are. Socialism never seemed to us very different from common sense. We preferred Gladstone to Disraeli. If I ever got above myself Denis would say *Encore un faiseur de paradoxes*. The events that marked us were the Suez adventure, which we thought incomprehensible and wicked, and the Hungarian revolution, after which I remember that the Oxford communist party, which had seven members all said to be in love with the same young comrade, went into a rethinking session of many hours, and in the end dissolved itself. Karl Marx I think we thought of as the most brilliant political journalist in the nineteenth century, a very good read but no source of light. All the same I read *Das Kapital* almost at a sitting to my own amazement, since it used to be called a difficult, obscure book, by those who feared it I dare say; I found nearly all of it easy going and well argued, but it had as little effect on me as Thomas More's *Utopia*. I was not really interested in reconstructing the world, only in what made my fellow-citizens tick. Engels on the English poor and Lukács on Walter Scott thrilled me more than Marx had ever done. Lenin I distrusted and Stalin I loathed. We took the revelations of the Twentieth

Party Congress as evidence for Russian states of mind; about the nature of Stalin's power we had never had any illusion. We were just a group of old-fashioned, Christian do-gooders, nourishing a small flame of romantic rage in our hearts.

Denis had very strong views about some things. He taught history for nearly twenty years at the National University in Dublin. He is dead now, but in his lifetime he was the only Englishman I ever knew who really understood Ireland, temperamentally, historically and actually. His wisdom on the subject was simple and alarming. When I came to him full of sociological theories about the ossification of ideas in a declining economy, he said he thought the troubles depended on sectarian religious education. If one side thinks the person across the street will go to hell, and that person thinks that you on this side are the devil and do the devil's work, trouble will come. That must be part of the truth, must it not? Why has no government the courage to abolish sectarian religious education in Northern Ireland? And everywhere else? All the same, I can remember a Vicar of Spelsbury who used to preach to the village about the Whore of Babylon clothed in scarlet and seated on seven hills. He was an Ulsterman and a good friend of mine. No one in Spelsbury took any notice. If the only trouble in Ireland were religion, tempers would surely have cooled by now, at least between atheists.

The landscape of Britain as we saw it was almost always a melancholy spectacle, however much we delighted in green grass and ragged hedges. Our feelings about the ruins of monasteries, about abandoned mines, ancient British camps or the White Horse on his hill-top were not sentimental or confused; they were quite sharp and real. It is intolerably sad to read the British countryside; it is like reading the *Iliad*. It is like those lines of Virgil where the ancient trees come crashing down, you can smell the foliage and the timber, birds fly up in a panic, and all this wood is going to burn, to consume the body of a young man freshly dead. There are still flowers you can find growing today in any hedge in England that take their names from the Danish wars: dwarf elder, pasque flower, fritillary, Dane's blood, Daneweed.

How they got those names is a matter for conjecture. Exotic beauty may have suggested a strange origin. Fritillaries, those purple and white checked meadow bell-flowers which now grow mostly in Magdalen Meadows, though they grew in meadows at Ruislip in my childhood, used to be called hanging bells of sodom, and up skirts. The pasque flowers growing on the Devil's Dyke and Fleam Dyke may have looked to our ancestors like memorials, as the poppies of Flanders did to our fathers. Dwarf elder was once called walwort, the stranger's or the enemy's flower, or perhaps the slaughter flower. The Danes were mythical, half forgotten, by the time walwort became Daneflower. And yet the bitter recollection of those wars lasted. When a Viking was caught he was skinned, and his skin was nailed to the church door. Justifiably, in my opinion. In the course of time, scholars had begun to deny that this ever happened, but in the last twenty years four or five church doors have been found in eastern England with human skin still sticking to them.

The new orthodoxy about the Vikings is to say they were traders and settlers; they were nothing but a people of exquisite art and innocent rustic culture. Certainly they settled far inland. Their sculpture where it was based on wood carving and their architecture when it was based on boat building, a wooden church being a kind of ship with the ship's weather vane stuck up on a spire, are certainly fine. But they were slavers and pirates and burners of villages. After a long morning in the wonderful Viking Art exhibition at the British Museum in 1980, with my head whirling with marvels, the crowded treasures, the long lines of the keels and whole forgotten styles and buried generations of which I knew nothing until that day, I went downstairs to cool my head among the manuscripts; and my eye fell on the work done by those monks the Vikings massacred. Absolutely nothing that the Vikings ever produced was worth one page of it. At least that was the strong impression that sabotaged my reasoning. One must qualify it by adding that both in London and at York two years later, the more humble an object was, the more impressive it was: ships' keels and their glittering weather vanes, a row of gloomy saints' faces cut like simple drawings on a flat board and found in Iceland, the whalebone ironing boards from the graves of Norwegian working women.

At the York exhibition one had the unique opportunity to see all together many monuments of stone from small, obscure, widely-scattered places which I had longed to see for twenty years. They would have taken half a year's continuous work to track down and visit in their old homes; it takes a lifetime to discover British antiquities. Denis and I used to assume in our Oxford days that life was going to be more adventurous and more open every year, as he became richer and I became more free. In the end one would have crisscrossed every moor and mountain, every green lump and bump and mouldering churchyard in Britain. And our memories would always be perfect, the notebooks would simmer on our bookshelves and swell in our coat pockets. All scholars are gypsies in their way.

Well may the reader ask how a classical scholar and a young clergyman, supposed to be obsessed with other interests, can have nourished such an illusion. There are several mitigating arguments. I had no idea then how much I depended on Denis for information, for encouragement, for discussion. I thought his territory was mine; I imagined one could master British antiquities in one's spare time. In my own subject, I thought I had no future; I was conscious of not being good enough to go on. It is not really possible to know a dead language. Only as a poet I was more than half inclined to abandon English and take to Latin. That would hardly reduce my likely number of readers and it might improve my Latin; it offered a dusty, perfectly private immortality, like Mr Scott-King's, a suitable ambition. I was argued out of my position by Julian Mitchell with stern brows. Another point in my favour is that I was invalided out of orthodox classical studies by being run over by a car.

Denis and I were exploring the Thames towpaths as far as Abingdon. It was a typical late autumn, early winter walk, the paths were muddy and the fields were flooded, but the wild swans and the dead leaves and the blustering wind transfigured the harmless Thames into an older and more powerful river. I once travelled with an old man on a train who was Master of some college beagles before the 1914 war. They got onto the scent of a stray stag and pursued it across the swollen Thames into the overgrown fields on the Oxford side; he had to swim across after them. Nothing as interesting happened to us, unfortunately. Simply the light began to fail, so we struck across country to find a road. We got dirtily but not unhappily lost, and by the time we got past Bagley Wood and started down Boar's Hill, the night was sooty dark. You could see the lights of Oxford glittering below, through a gap in the hedge. This gap was fatal. A little old lady in a little old car, being distracted by the lights, ran me over at a place where there was no pavement. I remember waking on my back on the tarmac and wondering why there were dead leaves in my bed. For the next two years I had concussion. No one expected me to work, least of all at Byzantine Greek, onto which I was shifted for a kind of rest cure. I read English medieval chronicles and seventeenth-century antiquaries to my heart's content. Denis and I corresponded in the prose styles of Clarendon or Izaak Walton or Charles I. I sat for afternoons on end in Bodley reading Drayton's *Poly-Olbion*, a voluminous and crazy topographic poem about England. Maybe I wanted to rival it, or translate it into Latin.

Medieval Greek added a sense of tragedy in ballads and epic poetry in another language. Denis and I both knew by then that the rhythm of real history is tragic, and we both sought in epic poetry for the only kind of expression of reality we completely respected. I must use the phrase epic poetry here more widely than I like to use it today, after twenty-five more years of similar study. It will have to include Homer, *Beowulf*, the *Song of Roland*, *The Seafarer* and *The Wanderer*, the *Passion* narrative of the gospels, and probably *In Parenthesis* by David Jones. Even the *Anglo-Saxon Chronicle* breaks into lamenting poetry. Many years have passed and many hours of reading been consumed in vain, before I could find my way alone through the intricacies of Dark Age history, but in a few lines of poetry and in certain landscapes, in almost every English landscape well meditated, one can get the feel of things.

Gazing at places is never a short cut to what happened in history, but a sense of place, of the small scale of the bright green ramparts, the dry, cracked tongues of the forest still stretching out, the flowering weeds, the lapwings in sunlight, the murmurations of starlings, an accurate sense of place is the fruit of a lifetime of patient scholarship. But our minds are discursive, our lives are not devoted to the past, we are not hermits of antiquity. What tells us most about the past is poetry. Denis once gave me a copy of *Waltharius*, a poem about Walter of Aquitaine, written in Latin by a Swiss monk around 930 AD. Versions of that exist in Anglo-Saxon, about 1000 AD, and in German and in Polish; its first, lost original was an epic poem in Bavarian. Its great king is Attila the Hun. I could no longer think that true epic stopped with Homer. There is something more terrifying, more cold-blooded, more cruel and at the same time braver in Anglo-Saxon heroic poetry than either the *Chronicle* or the abandoned strong places, or even the desolate burial mounds would lead you to expect.

That age was a world of chaos and dark storms. Saint Patrick complained of British slavers working the Irish coast. The Irish raided into Wales and the Scottish islands. Saint Fintan, who died in 879 AD, was taken from Leinster and sold as a slave in Orkney. On a gravestone in the Isle of Man, a wolf chews up a hero. There are figures of shadow, and vital episodes overgrown with legend. What lies behind Brendan's sea-journey, or the story of Ailbe, suckled by a she-wolf, who retired from this world to a Land of Youthfulness and Refreshment? The sea reveals less than the land, it is more enigmatic because it changes so constantly. One might think it had swallowed its old islands.

> There was no sound there but the slam of waves
> along an icy sea. The swan's blare
> my seldom amusement; for men's laughter
> there was a curlew call, there were the cries of gannets,
> for mead-drinking the music of the gull.
> . . . Now come thoughts
> knocking my heart, of the high waves,
> clashing salt-crests I am to cross again.

The small stone ruins of the earliest human occupation of St Kilda, which must I suppose be the remotest of all the British islands, far out beyond the Hebrides in Atlantic weather, suggest that the graves of the first pastoral settlers were in the shape of small boats dug into the ground, shallow-keeled and ghostly, built of big stones. The famous image of the soul that Bede records, a bird flying in from the dark night outside into the light of a great hall, and then flying out again, is terribly true of Anglo-Saxon history. Small, aggressive settlements of raiders or colonists, and then the denser intenser raids like heavy rain: the double role of the German mercenary soldiers left by Rome: the heavy push of Anglo-Saxon against old British place names and river names: and then the years and years of mutual slaughter. At last the christening of the English, by austere monks with heaven in their eyes, and then the beautiful culture that was not going to live long. Then the Danes and then the Normans. Northern England was half Danish by 1066. Harald of Norway might as easily have taken England as William of Normandy. Yet by the twelfth century a boy in Whitby called Tostig was so much laughed at for his Viking name he had to change it. He ended as a saint on the island of Farne, the place where Vikings first struck. He lived there under a Jewish name acceptable to Christians: Bartholomew.

CHAPTER SIX

The Western Flames

> Arrogant, lean, unvenerable, he
> Still turns for comfort to the western flames
> That glitter a cold span above the sea.
>
> Graves on Bridges

ONE WINTER EVENING toward the end of my time at Oxford, my poet friend Julian Mitchell produced a brother called Tony who took us both to see *Cymbeline* at Stratford. The production was both romantic and jolly, with long cotton wool beards and Strawberry Hill Gothick architecture. We drank delicious claret for dinner and laughed at the play more than Shakespeare or the producer intended, but the lyric about the all-dreaded thunderstone was perfect, which was all that mattered to me. Julian concentrated on 'Enter Jupiter armed with a thunderbolt, mounted on an eagle. The ghosts cower.' We drove back to Oxford through long lakes of groundmist that lay in every hollow, with the car plunging into them like a submarine.

Tony drove at what felt like five hundred miles an hour. I had made a new friend. He had been at Cambridge, at King's, where he became a refugee from the upper classes, and developed a passion for local British antiquities which was not well rewarded by the examiners in archaeology. His obsessions were aesthetic, and he let them rule his life. He was now in the wine trade; he hunted and went to grand dances with eyes full of curiosity. It was his boast that he could hunt his way, dance his way, or sell his way into almost any house in

England, and his life for years had been seriously organized around his passion for English country house architecture.

It was Tony Mitchell who in 1964 produced the National Trust atlas, which is little more than the formal publication of a long series of his privately annotated maps. He was the ideal new friend for me at that time. I went from Oxford to teach for two years in Lancashire, leaving London, and the swallows swooping through Euston arch, as if it were for ever. The awful first sight of northern industrial landscape around Warrington as one still saw it then, sprawling and unreformed, the discoloured slag heaps and the abandoned cotton mills and the terraced houses, struck a chill into my heart, and yet one was attracted as well, by the strangeness and decayed beauty; it seemed very far from London. Stonyhurst, where I went to teach, was even stranger and much lonelier and colder, and less beautiful. Yet who should be staying in the next town, selling wine and spying out the countryside, but Tony Mitchell on a northern tour.

He saved my life really, by anchoring my interest from the first week deep in that misty fell landscape, just before the bad weather closed in. Stonyhurst is an old Elizabethan forest castle that was smartened up in a severe style under James II, and extended into an elephantine public school in the nineteenth century. It stands near the foot of Longridge Fell, a huge whale-back with some pine trees and abandoned quarries; on the other side it looks towards Pendle, a clear silhouette shaped by the last ice age. The meandering border between Lancashire and Yorkshire is only a mile or so away. The local accent is like the voice of curlews. The local river is the Hodder, but as the proverb says, 'the Hodder, the Calder, the Ribble and the rain meet together in Mytton plain.' The disadvantage of Stonyhurst as a place is that it lies on and mostly consists of millstone grit, a heavy and unlovely stone which makes for grim piles of architecture and a lack of fine detail. Oxford by contrast seems to be built of antique ice cream and to decay as easily. But just beyond Longridge Fell lies the Trough of Bowland, a limestone landscape of amazing variety. From the top of Longridge the limestone country looks like the promised land. Come to that, on a clear summer's evening you can just make out the distant twinkling of Blackpool from up there.

From Stonyhurst in an hour or so you can get up into the best part of the Pennines, to Ingleborough and Malham, where we looked for cranesbill and the other special flowers of that amazing limestone scar. Ingleborough must be everyone's more or less favourite hill who knows it. I have seen it now in every weather; the cave systems inside it are almost more thrilling than the big shoulder of hillside. I used to take boys there to creep along the beds of underground streams, through cracks in rocks and stone holes like postboxes. The temperature hardly alters underground, but a sudden heavy thunderstorm can drown a gallery and flood a cavern in an hour or less. It is a long time ago now, but I still recall the weak, yellowish torchlight on the cave walls, and the waxen look of the stalactites like a sickness of the limestone.

Stonyhurst itself as the long Lancashire winter shut down on it was to me a chamber of echoes and forebodings. My colleagues were nervous of the world, and the world was distant. The boys felt abandoned; I felt hungry. The school was in a crisis of old-fashioned and new-fashioned ideas, all equally smeared over with a stiff appearance of virtue. I do not remember anyone at that time who was really happy there, except one or two very old men who had gone tranquilly crazy, and measured their happy footsteps boiled egg by boiled egg towards the looming battlements of heaven. One sweet old man whose lifework was measuring phenomenal downpours of rain for the Stonyhurst Observatory fell dead at the end of the Hallelujah Chorus when the school sang the *Messiah*. A member of my own generation, lost in the labyrinth on his first night, came upon a very old Jesuit indeed, a skull with spectacles as it were, in the petrological museum at midnight, busily polishing an ostrich egg. The boys got whatever education that kind of place has to offer, which is intellectually better and morally more painful than you might think. Their principal highway was an endlessly long gallery going nowhere, densely decorated with the heads of strange animals shot by old Stonyhurst boys. The masters, or those of them disinclined for rugby football, tramped away long afternoons through the bracken, tracking streams to their source, listening to sheep and the rustle of water. All that I learnt at Stonyhurst of any value, and I sometimes thought then all that anyone learnt, was what the landscape had to teach.

It was wild, cold, scarcely inhabited. Small wonder that the insides of houses were so over-cosy, the weather outside being so grim. There exists a special Lancashire melancholy which I have never seen elsewhere except in Sweden. Is that a matter of tribal character, or does it come from the climate? Tony Mitchell had among his jobs in the late fifties to market a drink called B and B, which was brandy and benedictine ready mixed. The highest intake of benedictine per head in Great Britain was at Bolton and its neighbour towns, near Stonyhurst. It was very sweet and very strong I suppose. Candy is dandy but liquor is quicker, and benedictine combines the advantages. By this time my own quarrel with the Jesuits and with myself, which I no longer mistook for a quarrel with God, had gone so far that I kept a supply of brandy in my room in a bottle labelled rust-remover, among some ropes and axes belonging to the boy scouts. I spent many, many hours keeping the boy scouts happy in and out of woods and rivers. They represented an alternative way of life for boys out of love with the orthodox ways of spending the afternoon; they were innocent creatures whom I came to like.

In the summer one had to take them somewhere. I took them to the Isle of Man, and once to a pleasant field by the River Eden, not far from Hadrian's Wall, and once to Scotland. For me the trip to Scotland was the most thrilling. After a year in Lancashire, a strong impression of northern life, and even a long day spent on the Wall where it wound its slow way across hill country, I was extremely curious about Scotland. I took a week based in a tiny clapper-boarded hotel overlooking the harbour at Mallaig, to see what I could organize. Mallaig was never a big place; it was created by the railway, late last century, and as the railways die, places like Mallaig at the far end of them have little future. By comparison to the bustle of Oban, Mallaig is a small village smelling badly of fish. There I worked for a time on a timber boat, loading and unloading trunks of pine trees between Mallaig and Knoydart. Knoydart in the late fifties was an enormous estate approachable by no road. It was a large knob that showed up on the map of Scotland. The owners had blown up the drover's track that used to function once as a coastal road, and Knoydart was a vast reserve for stalking and fishing and privacy.

It took three days to walk across from end to end. As you walked, you passed the ruins of crofters' cottages stubbed out like stone cigarette ends. Knoydart was an estate where depopulation had been actively encouraged. It had changed hands since then; it belonged in my day to a Conservative Member of Parliament for Hampshire. I remember that when I returned by arrangement with the gaggle of boys, we passed a Cabinet Minister fishing for trout or salmon. It was Buchan country. Knoydart was a revelation to me of how wild the landscape can be within Britain. Unless I am mistaken, it was still true in the fifties that the deer migrated more or less freely across Scotland every year, so that different estates had their best shooting at different seasons. Now having come close to being wiped out, all kinds of game are spreading once again into western Scotland through the glossy pelt of Forestry Commission trees. In the same way I remember it was said at Stonyhurst that the curlews had crossed the Pennines and come as far as Longridge only during the 1939 war. Yet they must once have been there in the past. What was it brought them back? The migrations of birds are only less painful than those of mankind in these islands.

The Western Islands of Scotland are not the isolated, traditional places one might imagine. They are not simple. What survives there does so almost by chance, like the colonies of rare seabirds that throng like wild bees in the crannies of the rockface. They are like rockpools really. Irish and Pictish and Scandinavian, Catholic and Calvinist and tribal Scotland are all represented. Every tide that has washed over the islands has left something of itself. The Scandinavian place names are often attached to landmarks, or rather to seamarks, that can be seen from a distance.

I have once helped to navigate a yacht round the British coast, which gave one a strong sensation of what those early navigations must have been like. She was newly built and still mastless; we were taking her round under engine from Liverpool to the Isle of Wight to have her mast stepped, but her compass was wild, having been fitted close to a sheet of non-demagnetized steel, so being mastless and ill-balanced, she heaved and screwed about like a wallowing animal. The coast of Wales and the Channel coast loomed and gloomed inscrutably; I recollect mistaking Torquay for a liner showing all its lights. The Channel was infested with enormous tankers like heavy trains unable to pull up. The safest way to steer was by the stars, which at least moved very slowly. Islands and coastal mountains stay the same of course, but dawn and the first clear glimpse of one's whereabouts can be an anxious moment, particularly if what one sees is a perfect, perfectly empty disc of sea, a circular horizon in all directions. I have seen that only twice in my life, but one of the times was in the English Channel, when that yacht's engine had failed and we lay wallowing.

On our Scottish adventure we visited the Isle of Rhum, arriving there in some kind of enormous motorboat, past the ominous dark mountains on Skye and the odd-shaped silhouette of Eigg. The idea was to help put rings on the feet of seabirds, a task that calls for many hands. The Isle of Rhum had at that time the biggest colony of Manx shearwaters outside Russia. I have seen them off their old home in the Isle of

Man, but very few. Their broken-off cry once heard is unforgettable; they travel the oceans of the world, hunting low down over the surface of waves like small packs of flying hounds, but to breed they return to the Isle of Rhum. On dusky, foggy nights they come in crying out of the night onto a certain mountainside, and their young hear them and creep out of hiding from among the stones. The night we chose was alight with the brightest moonlight. When we got to the mountaintop one could see for some twenty miles; the entire sea was glittering like a dancing floor. Hardly one bird fluttered down.

Although I have seen a lot of Scottish islands since then, not one was more memorable. On Jura the deer far outnumber the people, which is surely how things ought to be. The Paps of Jura are two fine little mountainous cones of stone. The northern tip of that island was George Orwell's last refuge, where he lived on rabbit and lobster. I met a neighbour, I think a retired Eton housemaster's wife, who remembered him as an odd kind of man, sitting at his kitchen table on a sort of camp stool and smoking innumerable French cigarettes. How strange it is that one should go so far and feel so much more at home with this bony-faced literary exile from London than one does with the whole intervening population of England and Scotland. Yet I should admit that was my case, because one of the principal benefits of travel is that it teaches you who you are. On the Isle of Rhum we lay on the rocks and sang to the seals, who barked back at us, shaking their moustaches. We departed at the crack of dawn in grandeur on a MacBrain's steamer that must have collected the post.

That island was like Prospero's; it was too good to be true. One could hardly feel at home there unless one had the boyish concentration of a naturalist. The last laird's or squire's house seemed a monument of futility. His ruined garden had a little humpbacked bridge in the Japanese taste. Whatever islanders were left lived elsewhere I think, in a small fishing village on the far side. Three splendid mountains lay stretching their beautiful flanks, and that was all. What kind of life can there ever have been in the Hebrides? In the eighteenth century, islanders still died of the common cold when a stranger landed. Slave ships and pirates were as common then as birds of prey to this day; no life can have been more innocent or less easy than that of the Hebrideans. It is often said that the Irish as the English first met them were retarded; they were relics of the Iron Age, because of all Britain Rome had left only Ireland untouched. The Scottish islanders until the day before yesterday were the people of a world at least equally remote from ours. They were as wild as the colonies of sea birds off which they lived.

Consider this, by Martin Martin, a medical man and an agent of the Macleods of Skye, on the subject of St Kilda in 1698. 'The *Solan* Geese have always some of their Number that keep Centinel in the Night-time, and if they are surprized, (as it often happens) all that Flock are taken one after another; but if the Centinel be awake at the approach of the creeping Fowlers, and hear a noise, it cries softly, *Grog*, *Grog*, at which the Flock move not; but if the Centinel see or hear the Fowler approaching, he cries quickly *Bir*, *Bir*, which would seem to import danger, since immediately after, all the Tribe take Wing, leaving the Fowler empty on the Rock, to return home *re infecta*, all his Labour for that Night being spent in vain. Here is a large Field of Diversion for *Apollonius Tyanaeus*, who is said to have Travelled many Kingdoms over, to Learn the Language of Beasts and Birds.' I was unable to resist transcribing the last sentence with the rest, because it so nicely situates Martin Martin, who already observes both birds and islanders from a pretentious distance.

It is sometimes claimed that what was done to the Scots was done by themselves. It would be truer to say that they were treated by the Normans just as intolerably as the Irish were treated, or would have been so had their innermost mountains not been so daunting. The earliest history of Scotland is utterly misty because of those same mountains. All that survives is a glimpse of nomads, the remnant of a dugout canoe, broken blades of a few stone butchers' axes among the skeleton of a stranded whale. No one knows when the Gaelic language arrived in Scotland. In the first century AD, the Romans had a tribal map which makes far more sense of the coast and the great headlands than it does of inner Scotland, but the same can be said of maps of Scotland and Ireland down to the sixteenth century. The border area of England and Scotland, with its constant local warfare until the two kingdoms joined under the crown, and the special architecture of its castles and shielings fortified against raiding, was set up by the Romans in the third century as a breakwater against unconquerable mountain tribes. Genocide had been tried and failed. The migration of Gaels, the invasions from Scandinavia, from England and Germany, were not like tides of the sea that passed over Scotland and withdrew. The mountains would not permit that. The Scotland of the early Middle Ages was a patchwork of aggressive small kingdoms. The clan system is a fiction that weaves that patchwork into one thing. The old northern Scots, the people called the Picts, disappeared utterly. Norman infiltration from the south carried with it a branch of the English language, but for hundreds of years even that stopped short of the mountains. Orkney was Norse from the annihilation of the Picts until 1469. It was a famous slaving centre. The massacre of Glencoe happened under the British monarchy, but it could not have happened in England.

The Welsh had suffered it all earlier. That interesting double-faced clergyman Gerald of Barry, who is perhaps a better because a more naïve historian than is always admitted, was both a Norman, looking for promotion in the church and prepared to go to Rome three times in pursuit of the archbishopric he never achieved, and a true Welshman descended from Welsh princes. His description of Wales makes Welsh attitudes clear enough. The forests are places of ambush and the passes between mountains are ominous; the waterbirds on the lakes know that the Welsh are true kings of Wales. The lakes are full of fish and magic: a lake of one-eyed fish and another with a floating island. Snowdon, the snow-mountains, has grazing enough for all the flocks in Wales. The numerous Welsh saints, like the ancient Welsh heroes, are more vengeful than those of other Christians. Rambones are oracular. Horns and bells, which are pleasingly called *bangu*, are sacred. I think I am right in saying that bells in Rumanian are *clangu*. Wales has mysterious lonely chapels of ivy and moss, and sacred fish in remote rivers. The fish stories are even weirder than the dog stories. The nightingales are too wise to enter such a country. The fairies speak in Greek.

Small wonder that Gerald with his double blood wanted to rule in Wales, if only as a priest. He believed, perfectly properly, that St David's ought to be independent of Canterbury. But he travelled with the Archbishop in Wales to raise men for the crusades; he had travelled in Ireland as an attendant on King John, an observer with Norman eyes. The power for which Gerald of Wales was ambitious was defined for him by the Norman state and by the papacy. Being Welsh was a kind of suffering, it was being backward, magical, a shepherd on a mountain, being thought a kind of savage and treated so by the master race. The Welsh gentry still go to Shrewsbury to school. Children around Holywell who speak only Welsh until they go to school, have to learn English to manage on the buses. Later, they are often ashamed of their Welsh, proud of their English. The same kind of thing is true in bilingual parts of Scotland. Gerald says 'The English are striving for power, the Welsh for freedom. The Welsh want only to find refuge in the woods, the mountains and the marshes. The memory which they will never lose of their old greatness may well kindle a spark of hatred in the Welsh.' He ends with the reply of an old man at Pencader who fought under Henry II against Wales in 1163: 'My Lord King, this nation is now harassed, weakened and decimated by your soldiers, as it often was by others in the past, but it will never be utterly destroyed by the wrath of man, unless it is punished at the same time by the wrath of God. Whatever else happens, I do not think that on the Day of Dreadful Judgement any race other than the Welsh, or any other language will give answer to the Supreme Judge of All for this small corner of the earth.'

I got to know Wales more gradually and therefore more intimately than Scotland, through a series of compulsory annual holiday based on the outskirts of Barmouth, and later through spending a year in North Wales. The first attraction of Richard Wilson to me must have been that he painted the unlikely shapes and lakes of Cader Idris, still to me the most moving because the most familiar of all mountains. In the same way I discovered John Parker because he painted the long waterfall of Rhaeadr Ddu, the heavenly long meandering waterfalls that drop like the grace of heaven down a mile or two miles of hillside under oak trees above Maentwrog. The topmost of the falls are the most beautiful: three or four crisscrossing mares' tales of white water course down over tall rocks with a rainbow caught in the spray. John Parker's Rhaeadr Ddu is in the National Library of Wales, who print a postcard of it. I have another painting of the same falls behind the desk where I write, thinly and boldly done, mostly in blue and white. It is so austere as to be almost Chinese, profoundly exhilarating and light-spirited. John Parker's oak branches and solid water enter deeply into the nature of the place. In this other painting nature has become spirit, but it has an earthliness you can breathe.

As I grew older I became more and more deeply in love with my friends, and with provincial Britain. Our training was so long and dull I lost interest in my own future. In the course of time I contracted the habit of trying to induce some non-Jesuit friend to stay in the neighbourhood whenever I found myself in any remote or interesting spot. I came back from that first visit to Scotland by a long, slow train journey, having no more responsibility for the boys beyond Fort William. I travelled south with Denis; we stayed the night in a vast and dignified hotel where there was nothing acceptable to drink but champagne. We were lucky in the vintage and also dog-tired. I fell asleep almost before getting into bed, and dreamed of deer high up on the mountains in early summer, wallowing in the last of the snowdrifts. It was the first time for weeks I had slept in sheets and they were blessedly cold.

The climax of the last of those Welsh holidays was the night we climbed Cnicht. Denis Bethell and Tony Mitchell were both in Wales, Denis and I at Barmouth, and Tony I think at the Portmeirion Hotel, which I have heard unkindly described as a Butlin's designed by the Sitwells. To me it was a paradise of out-of-date smartness and extravagant beauty. A Georgian Gothic façade from Bristol, an Austrian chapel roofed with green canoe canvas, a plaster Shakespeare leaning from a balcony, a Welsh cottage with a perfect garden, the tired summer sky, the encircling woods, the intelligent floodlights. It was *urbs in rure*. Add the people, for whom one felt a strong affection, and what could have seemed a more blissful refuge from my scrubbed boarding house? Add also the champagne and the fresh grilled lobster. Portmeirion was no threat to me as a clergyman; it did not offer a way of life.

Across the estuary from Portmeirion the pure thin grass of Talsarnau, which means the treading stones, trails down to the water. The estuary is broad and shallow and sandy, though the tide comes in and out fast. In the distance you can see sand dunes. One foursquare white house with one outlying white cottage stand close to the water's edge. I mean the water's edge at high tide, because at low tide one can cross over the half mile of the estuary, from sand bar to sand bar, hardly getting wet above the knee. This house is Mor Edrin; it belonged then to Richard Hughes the novelist and his wife Frances; there they brought up their children, barefooted, sea-going and mountain-climbing. He read the Bible in Welsh at village services, and entertained magnificently in a house where even the tables looked wind-scoured and sea-scoured. Frances painted and gardened. For years she painted the sea, and then for years it was waterfalls, which gave her in the end very bad rheumatism. It is her Rhaeadr Ddu which hangs now behind my table.

Richard Hughes sometimes used to sit under a portrait of himself by Augustus John. By some mysterious transformation it looked as wind-scoured and as sea-scoured as everything else. I cannot remember the windows, but more light came in through them than would have done elsewhere. It was the kind of light that would pick a bone perfectly clean. They were the wisest friends I had ever had. They were profoundly wild and tolerant.

In the good old days, parties of young girls in ball gowns with their skirts held up above their knees used to cross over at low tide from Mor Edrin to grand dances at Portmeirion. I remember well how Tony Mitchell and I, being late for dinner, attempted to imitate that crossing. On our own we might have found the way, but Frances insisted on sending a girl of sixteen to be our guide. We were both wearing suits and I had an umbrella. She led us where there was nothing to do but swim; had we gone astray on our own, we might have removed our trousers; as it was we must ford the flooding water however we could. I carried my umbrella between my teeth and paddled like a dog. Someone at Portmeirion had recently made the mistake of ordering seven cases instead of seven bottles of pink champagne for some reception, so the staff were under orders to entertain with nothing else. I sat on the floor, oozing seawater, and the champagne also fizzed and spilt. But the night that Denis and Tony and I climbed up Cnicht was something else again.

An old painter called Jim Wiley, whose usual address was Numero Zero, Place de la Kasbah, Tangier, and who was one of the founders of Portmeirion, still used to visit there every year. The architect, Clough Williams Ellis, was his old friend. Jim Wiley used to run the Northgate Café in Cornmarket Street, Oxford when it was the Moorish Tea Rooms in the 1920s, pioneering Bakst ballet designs as domestic decorations. He it was who told me about the ghosts in Cwm Croesor, the valley below Cnicht. You could sometimes hear the tramping of men and the creak and rumble of waggons, but you never understood their language. It was a Roman legionary road. The Hughes family had lived there, but they were driven out by various ghosts. A figure like a badly-dressed jockey constantly opened their gate for invisible coaches to go by, letting out Frances's hens. Clough himself, whose wedding present from the Welsh Guards was an artificial ruin, had built his garden with a view of Cnicht like a perfectly framed picture, a mountain like a shark's fin. Cwm Croesor lay below it.

On the night in question, our last evening after ten days or so of Welsh perambulations, as far south as Strata Florida and as far north as those lunar mountaintops of the Glyder range that peer northwards at Anglesey and southwards at Snowdon, we were due to dine at Portmeirion with Michael Duff, a figure of bizarre grandeur and preposterous humour whom I greatly loved. He was very rich; he owned the slate mines of Blaenau Festiniog and most of Snowdon. He was also Lord Lieutenant, and insisted on the hotel flying his personal standard if he dined there. He was a son of Lady Juliet Duff, whose zany charm he inherited and somehow increased. It goes without saying that such a man was deeply sad: the kind of sadness that envious and silly people often mistake for boredom. It also goes without saying that dinner was fresh lobster and ever-fresh champagne. Our scheme was for Denis and me to walk back alone in bright moonlight up Cwm Bychan and over the mountains, which between us we knew well. But dinner was terribly late, we were in dangerously high spirits, and Tony Mitchell feared a disaster. We compromised by agreeing to climb Cnicht, which none of us had ever done before, and then driving home.

For more than a day or two Tony and I had been arguing on and off about the landscape. The core of this straying, disconnected discussion was that Shelley had advised Mr Maddox, creator of wonderful, geometric Portmadoc, the next town to Portmeirion, how to drain a huge, estuarine valley and make hundreds of acres more of grazing land for those little black

Welsh cattle with suspicious eyes, for which the English market word used to be Welsh runts. This improvement really happened, making impractical Shelley to my delight of all poets the one who has most affected British landscape, more than Pope or Shenstone and infinitely more than Shakespeare or John Clare. And more than Chaucer, even though his official job was clearing the tributaries that ran into the Thames at London. But Peacock, Shelley's friend, took an opposing view. He wrote a letter or published a pamphlet against this new scheme, and if I recollect our argument rightly, he wrote 'The everlasting hills remain, but gone is the evershining mirror which reflected them.'

Whether or not the little valley under Cnicht was really involved in that old controversy I am unable to say, but as we probed our way up it and finally abandoned the car, we continued to argue. I took Shelley's side, Tony Mitchell took Peacock's, and Denis laughed at both of us. We clambered from dewy field to dewy upper field through rainsoaked hedges. The sides of the mountain grew steeper. We encountered a little scree and some bushes, and came to rest under what seemed a high, rocky buttress. We might have given up but someone found a way round. Sometimes it is possible to climb a whole Welsh mountain on grass, by far the most dangerous way to do it, unless one is barefoot. I have come upon pieces of aeroplane embedded in the grassy wall. On the other hand I have also slid all the way down one of those massive grass ramparts on my backside incurring no injury except indelible blueberry stains, a sort of woad-like warpaint. We were suddenly on the top of Cnicht. As we looked down the estuary glittered. The valley was flooded again, and the water rippled with reflected moonlight. It was all an effect of the groundmist as we discovered, but that was a frightening moment.

There is a footnote to these Welsh amusements. Gerald of Barry on his journey 'crossed the Traeth Mawr and the Traeth Bychan', a big and a small arm of the sea, where two stone castles had been built. 'The one called Deudraeth belongs to the sons of Cynan and faces the northern mountains.' This must refer to the twelfth-century vallum lost in the woods above Portmeirion, and to the name Penrhyndeudraeth, the local village. A *traeth*, as Gerald notices, is an area of estuarine sand that the ebb tide leaves bare. In the last revision of his manuscript, Gerald confused his record by adding the names of two rivers which everyone agrees he put in the wrong place. But the big *traeth* was surely the one between Portmeirion and Mor Edrin, and the little one the Portmadoc estuary in its old state, before Shelley and Mr Maddox altered the landscape. 'The territory of Cynan, and especially Merioneth, is the rudest and roughest of all the Welsh districts. The mountains are very high, with narrow ridges and a great number of very sharp peaks all jumbled together in confusion.' It is pleasant to think of the Archbishop of Canterbury and the rest of them plucking up their skirts to cross over from the stepping stones near Mor Edrin, across the estuary to Portmeirion.

But nothing falls to pieces faster than a fantasy. Now Portmeirion is almost as dusty and out of fashion as the works of Gerald of Barry, Archdeacon of St David's in the twelfth century. He wrote of Bardsey island, still occupied at that time by non-Romanized Irish monks, that 'either because of its pure air, which comes across the sea from Ireland, or through some miracle by the holy saints who lived on it, no one dies on this island except of extreme old age, disease being almost unheard of. In fact no one dies at all, unless he is very old indeed.' The same is true to this day of the English Carthusians. Gerald and the Archbishop did not adventure offshore. Maybe he was thinking of his native island of Barry.

These long digressions in Scotland and Wales did not represent any digression of interest to me. After two years teaching, I had to face four more at Heythrop, reading theology. But once seen, these provincial wild places continued to exercise thought and imagination as one sat through endless lectures. I raised mine eyes unto the hills, whence came my salvation. They were chosen, or rather thrust on us as students, more or less for the purposes of a Victorian holiday. They were considered perfectly healthy except for the danger of death, and I did in fact have friends who were killed on mountains and drowned in beautiful rivers. It is strange how quickly the Victorians thought they had those places tamed. Hardly had the first artists, led by the watercolourists like light infantry, penetrated the last wildernesses of Britain, than it seemed to the Victorians that art was dominant there. Through their superior talents or the dark genius of romantic artists, whichever way you looked at it, the inward nature of Scotland and Wales seemed to belong to the art-loving English, just as certainly as the ground belonged to those who shot over it and the rivers to those who owned their fishing. In English law you can still own the bed of a river, or even half of the bed of a river. It is as if Wordsworth invented the Lakes, and Crabbe or perhaps Britten owned East Anglia.

But through living in places like Stonyhurst, and the village of Tremeirchion in Flintshire, where I spent 1964–5 as an apprentice priest at last, places originally chosen for remote refuges by a community used to persecution, some of us took in a strong feeling for the North and for the Welsh. I recollect several attempts to learn Welsh, more or less naïve and unsuccessful, including my own. One solemn-faced young man came home to tea full of curiosity about a new word that appeared on notices but never in a dictionary. It turned out to be budc, that is BUDC, Barmouth Urban District Council.

My own climax of attainment was a service at Tremeirchion attended by local people who were native Welsh speakers. I planned it with a friend, an old Christ Church man who became a Jesuit and is now I believe a happy low church Anglican clergyman. He was a highly nervous historian to whom I felt close because we shared two awful years at Stonyhurst, where the boys tied his shoelaces together and let off bombs under his desk. When the great moment came, he knew enough Welsh to read his way through the service, while

I could scarcely stumble through one prayer. All I could do was preach in English on a text from the *Song of Songs*, 'I have dried fruit and fresh fruit hung up behind the door,' on Welsh rural tradition. It was a gesture, but it set no river on fire.

Stonyhurst flinging as it did shades of the prison house upon the masters as well as the boys, we came to know well whatever natural and whatever archaeological features lay within ambitious walking distance. We had a good, and in some ways excellent Victorian library. I can assure less privileged readers that Philemon Holland's *Livy* and Dryden's *Virgil* are easier reading in the first edition. Hopkins, who worked once at Stonyhurst, seems to have procured *The City of Dreadful Night* when it came out. It did not matter much to me that D. H. Lawrence and The Modern Novel in general were kept in a special room available only to senior boys. By hindsight, and not for the same reasons, I even begin to see some sense, of a twisted kind, in that arrangement. But I had my own supply of novels, including the early books of my own friends. And for me the important shelf in the library was the one that sheltered Dugdale's *Monasticon*, the best reference book to the ruins of British monasteries that existed at that time, the masterpiece of the seventeenth-century antiquarian movement. We were willing to travel a long way to any ruin, we tramped the fells, and we studied Roman relics until we tired of them, which did not take very long.

The expectations early antiquaries had of Roman British ruins have scarcely been fulfilled. Only, being once imagined, they seeded into British earth through the fantasy of poets. In the seventeenth and eighteenth centuries this crop of Roman and Italian fantasy was harvested year after year: 'Large streets, brave houses, sacred sepulchers, Sure gates, sweete gardens, stately galleries.' British classical architecture of recent centuries is very much more attractive than the real ruins of Roman Lancashire. We did, on the other hand, get a grasp of industrial history, for which Stonyhurst is almost ideally placed. In small towns like Clitheroe you could see how poor and crowded streets overlay what had once been the divisions of fields. The wind on the castle howled like a harp. There were still cobblestones in Clitheroe and in Preston, and people still spoke about the clatter of wooden clogs on the cobbles every working morning until our lifetime. The old local song, 'Please do not burn our shithouse down,' still had an obvious social reality.

The Ribble and the Mersey were highroads of invasion at one time. There were two or three strange burials recorded on the Ribble of chiefs buried upright in their chariots, horses and all. So I recollect them, although I have never seriously studied the excavations, which must have been a long time ago if they got into any book I was reading in the 1950s. These burials date from the time of the first Roman invasions into England, maybe a little earlier or later, but before the Romans arrived so far North. The people concerned seemed to be Belgians. If that is right, it is another example of how wave followed wave of invasion, and how one wave overtook another. The Romans were only one more wave in a thousand years of tidal water.

It is natural to conjecture that many wild and strange ways of life must have been buried under what came later. A so-called civilized people fears and suppresses whatever is primitive. That divine right of the Romans to rule which the British fatally acknowledged and never quite forgot, to which they appealed against their later invaders, and which the Middle Ages and the Renaissance drank in from Virgil and from the pretensions of the papacy, has not a shred of historical validity. The same goes for the historical mission of Alfred. The same goes for the Normans, and in Scotland and Ireland for the Tudors. The disoriented and wicked civilizers pursue their moral betters. Our history in these islands is too tragical to think about. We have abandoned its reality, and taken to a myth which is useful for stabilizing the state.

Although I am no historian, and although the few years of reading that I undertook for this book faced me with many surprises, things half known or half remembered turning out to be the merest Christmas decorations covering solid walls of ignorance, I cannot avoid thinking now that the identification with Rome and with Caesar has done us terrible harm. It seems to have been accepted without question that Rome brought civilization and culture would then follow. Evolution was a cultural idea and an image of history long before Darwin. The British came to believe that Christianity had come to them from Rome, and that was no doubt a persuasive analogy. Christianity, like civilization, would follow the flag to Jerusalem and far beyond. It would follow avarice like a falling star far into the Atlantic and into the China Seas. Even Samuel Johnson's towering common sense found this kind of argument strong: 'No faction of Scotland loved the name of Cromwell, or had any desire to continue his memory. Yet what the Romans did to other nations, was in a great degree done by Cromwell to the Scots; he civilized them by conquest, and introduced by useful violence the arts of peace. I was told at Aberdeen that the people learned from Cromwell's soldiers to make shoes and to plant kail.'

When the British arrived in America, they felt at once a similarity of subject races between the ancient British and Pictish tribes and the American Indians. The two obvious things these very different peoples were thought to have in common were nakedness, which for Celtic people was a ritual thing and also their habit in battle, and tattooing, both of them sensitive subjects to this day. Why did the British settlers in Africa as late as the thirties take such a poor view of naked black bodies? They dressed up elaborately, they feared 'going native'. Africa shocked them both sexually and culturally. As for tattooing, there is a mysterious intercommunion of the tattooed. In Britain tattoos go so often with criminality that HM Prison Service offers long-term prisoners the free removal of their tattoos as an aid to respectability. I have seen in a small folklore museum in Cairo an old tattooist's display board with images that go right round the world. The ikonography of tattoos ought to attract a serious art historian.

In the Musée de l'Homme in Paris, where everything is subordinated to the conception of man in France as the masterpiece of mankind, and prehistoric man as the blood-brother of colonial man, 'savage' tattoos of human skin are shown in a glass case beside 'modern' tattoos: republican tattoos taken from those executed after the *Commune*. There is also a skeleton in a case called '*type litéraire, Duc de Saint Simon*', next to one called '*type criminel, Assassin du Général Kleber*'. These bones have recently been given a hand-written card to say they represent a theory now not generally held, which is a relief. It is interesting all the same that most of the collection was organized by the human evolutionist Teilhard de Chardin. The exhibition, at least as it was ten years ago, precisely fitted in with the views he expressed in letters about China and the Chinese. Civilization must come to them from Paris, and one could be civilized only by being colonized. The Chinese had no art.

We know about the analogy of Picts and Red Indians from John White who sailed on Raleigh's expedition to Virginia in 1585 and came home with Drake the next year. He went again in 1587 with an expedition of his own. That time he brought home an Indian whom he baptized at Bideford, but the Indian died. White spent five years or more in five attempts to colonize Roanoke Island; in 1590, the last time he went out, he saw smoke ascending from the woods, but when his sailors landed the colonists had vanished utterly. Thomas Harriot, another member of Raleigh's 1585 expedition, wrote an account which he published in 1588 in London. An engraver from Liège who was in London at the time, Dirk de Brie, the same artist who engraved Sidney's funeral procession in 1587, reprinted Harriot's book at Frankfurt in 1590, with engravings from the drawings of observed Indian life made by John White. As a kind of supplement, he also engraved John White's *Picts and Britons*, of which we have some original water-colours.

The Pictish warrior is a figure of deliberate ghastliness. The engraving slightly tones him down. He displays himself like a Greek athlete in a statue, weight all on one foot. He has a small shield, a pretty spear with a *fleur-de-lys* blade at one end and a knob at the other, a huge cutlass tied on with a rope, and the heads of two Elizabethan gentlemen, one of which he waves gently. He stands in an appetizing landscape ripe for colonization, with a ship under sail in the bay. In White's watercolour version everything is even more hideous: no landscape but a sandy ground, the face a livid bluish colour, the eyes ecstatic, blood dripping from the pole and unkempt head the savage holds. His tattooing is completely unreal; its effect is only to disguise his nakedness, since he is elaborately tattooed with a Venetian grotesque version of Roman armour, including a skirt tattooed on his thighs. There existed of course no real life model for a Pict. His sex does not appear unless one is looking for it. There is something effectively disgusting about him.

But John White also drew a Pictish princess, who tells another tale. In her original watercolour she has a Shakespearean beauty. One would certainly not see she was naked at first sight. As with the warrior, the torque she wears round her neck is like the collar of what seems her dress. She leans on an ornamental spear and wears a cutlass on a golden chain. Her whole body is covered with painted flowers like the finest white embroidered silk. Her hair falls in golden waves like a mermaid's. The tips of her breasts are the golden centres of roses, and what seem to be lilies sprout out of her sex. She stands in a nobleman's park with a country house behind her, like a figure imagined in *Cymbeline* or *A Winter's Tale*, or someone strayed out of a daring private masque. She represents the other side of the coin, the image of a naked woman. She is lovely, desirable, mythical. The flowers were painted on her by Jacques Le Moyne de Morgues, friend of Sidney, painter of *Le Clef des Champs*, and to my mind the most magical and fragrant painter of flowers in that startling century. He also drew in America, but that is another story.

In the end these English images of barbarity came full circle, and the Scots, more intensely after Culloden, but earlier also, were policed with a series of forts on land and with boats on the water, as if they were Indians and Loch Ness was one of the great American lakes. The soldiers were quite conscious of what they were doing. One of those Johnson met in 1773 had taken part in the Ohio expedition, and more than one of them had fought American Indians. The commander of the King's strongest fort in Scotland, who commanded Scots among others, just as the British forces in India included Indians, had risen to his rank through colonial experience. Peace must be imposed, woods and minerals exploited, civilization carried forward. Sitting in a remote stone school on the Lancashire fells, where the weather was so bad one could sometimes not see to the end of the avenue for a fortnight at a time, where the portraits of old boys with VCs, often posthumous, clustered on the dining-room walls, and the blood of the martyrs seemed to make gurgling noises in the chapel radiators, it was natural to meditate these evil themes. Stonyhurst in the late fifties posed questions like What has gone wrong? and What is our tradition, where does it come from? At that time these seemed to be practical questions, though now I think they are ghostly.

It was another epoch. When a boy stole a rifle from the armoury of the Stonyhurst Cadet Corps to give it to the IRA, we thought that was a joke. So it was, in the late fifties.

CHAPTER SEVEN

That Mystical Philosophy

> This is that mystical Philosophy, from whence no true Scholar becomes an Atheist.
>
> Browne, *Religio Medici*

FOR FOUR YEARS in the early sixties I sat down once again at Heythrop in North Oxfordshire, to study theology. Most of us were about thirty, we were already very tired of being students, and four years at that age, under those bleak conditions, is a long pull. No doubt theology is a confused subject in every age. In my time Thomas Aquinas, whose theological works were our standard textbooks in philosophy, was seldom mentioned in theological lectures. As for the learned foundations of the subject, one had to pursue those, if at all, on one's own. 'Ha, Mr Levi,' said Eduard Fraenkel one day in a bookshop, 'I see you sometimes visit our classical Hades. And how is theology?' 'Awful,' I replied. 'But the great Cappadocian Fathers?' 'Terrible.' 'Ah. Ah. And Augustine? Do you not think a great deal of Augustine is just belly ache?' 'Indeed I do.' 'And have you read *Hilarius De Virginitate*?' 'No, but I can imagine it.' 'It is not the obscene subject, but the disgusting prose style.' I found no theological professor I preferred to Fraenkel.

I saw something at times of Denis and of Tony Mitchell, I went often to Oxford or London, to museums and libraries, and explored the Cotswolds far more thoroughly than before. Religion for me was like a flock of birds moving across the winter fields and among the stony villages. Twenty years ago a way of life survived in villages that must have vanished by now altogether. In the big snow of one of those winters a squire on skis was taken for an apparition from the other world. In the summer, the country boys used to walk ten miles to a dance and ten miles home after it. You could still travel a long way across country and meet no one. You could swim naked in lonely rivers. You could bicycle safely at night from Chipping Norton to the Welsh coast. Canals were overgrown but there were still railways.

As I grew older I travelled constantly by rail, and spent time in more parts of England than it would serve any purpose now to record. The English Jesuits as they were in my time were a product of the railway age, in spite of their remote Elizabethan origins. Recusant houses of a ghostly beauty like Stonor among the beech woods, where Edmund Campion once hid, represented to most of us a tradition too romantic to be taken seriously. We yearned for cities and big towns, we ate sausages that tasted of railway soot, we were at home in the train. By our mid-thirties we knew more different areas of the British class system, more unplotted regions of it, than other citizens, and once we were ordained we began to accumulate a confidential insight into people's lives that few people are permitted. We knew where in England to expect incest, and where to be unsurprised by murder. It makes for a sad kind of wisdom, not at all like that of Chesterton's Father Brown, more like that of Simenon's Maigret, the melancholy knowledge of Paris.

I wish in a way I had made a new start in 1960, with a clear, secular field of study. In theology I read hugely and widely, but as a point of honour mostly outside the syllabus of our studies, which were still conducted at a nursery level. I was so freakish as to fail an exam here and there. It was not that I was a poet, but philosophy and the classics had made me unteachable. My future was already determined; I was meant to go back to Oxford as a professional classical scholar, and after some ups and downs that is what happened. But think of a new subject, as clear and fresh as grass; think of a subject almost scientific. Consider archaeology. At first sight it had the advantage of aking place in the open air, or in the museums where the nine nuses shouted for joy like the children of God.

The Roman archaeologist Richmond had a face like a Cox's apple, he was full of health, he beamed with cheerfulness. He vas the only person I knew in Oxford who always had time to top and chat in the street. I once attended a lecture by him in he fens not far from Cambridge. It rained heavily, while he opped up and down on top of a mighty dyke, and probed into orners of a fairly ordinary field of long grass. It was a splendid nd physically exhilarating performance, though it left some f the audience dampened both in spirit and in fact. Tom Brown Stevens of Magdalen, who abandoned Roman history o become presiding wizard of the Dark Ages was even jollier nd warmer than Richmond. As a teacher he was a pied piper, lord of misrule, and we adored him. He taught seventy hours week, and hunted on Saturdays.

But by then I had come to think of the Romans as a auseating people, partly through brooding and teaching bout them in Lancashire, partly through reading Mommsen's *History of the Roman Republic*, that monument of love-hate. They have made a desert and called it peace' seemed true to ne. Most of Roman recorded time was a process of decline of ne kind or another. The famous Northumberland wall was eautiful, but that was a product of the English landscape and he English weather. As a device it was unoriginal, being only a opy of the Great Wall of China, so Stevens said. Most Roman emains in England are miserable. On the final day of my first isit to Greece in 1963, after saying my goodbyes to the arthenon and the great Athenian museums, I went on board hip and read in *The Times* that English archaeologists were hrilled by their new discovery of three Roman military boot-uds, stuck into some very old mud in a road in Kent. A hotograph was appended. Maurice Bowra used to say nglish archaeologists were the only ones who were so vir-uous they preferred to dig where they wouldn't find anything. One does see what he meant.

When I went to see that great man about what I ought t
teach in Oxford, my academic record being as chequered as th
woods in autumn, he asked what I was really passionate abou
I stuttered a bit and came out with literature more than histor
Greek more than Latin except for Horace, and poetry mor
than prose, but also Greek vase painting which I loved becaus
Beazley made everyone love it. 'I see,' he said. 'Like me. Pot
and Poetry. Pots and poetry. No way to pay and promotion
Really the problem solved itself, because I got so ill in thos
Lancashire mists and rivers and those wet woods and col
rooms and North Oxfordshire fogs, that for years after that
had to go south in winter, so archaeology was the obviou
solution: some lonely fringe of archaeology where I coul
work on my own.

In a way I wish it had been English, in spite of never findin
anything. I have never in my life discovered anything i
England except one badly-made flint arrowhead nea
Chanctonbury Rings, that antique-looking wind-stunte
grove which was planted by a shepherd almost within livin
memory. Of course I was more passionate as a student abo
Greece and the Greek language and the Greeks than I wa
about humps and bumps and heavings of the English tur
Wishing those years away would be like cutting out one
heart. But what I read most in Athens was Shakespeare, and
have always been head over heels in love with the Englis
landscape. It was always there to come home to. It has nev
lost its mystery, its weather, its raw past. There were da
when after a hasty flight from the stony hillsides and the pin
flowering trees of the early Greek spring, England seeme
intolerably green. Standing under young horse chestnuts wa
like being imprisoned inside a greengage. Green salad was to
bright to eat. On other days there were woods and hilltops a
blue as ink. The whole sky towards Herefordshire was o
enormous wrestling-ground of giant white clouds, baroqu
heroes of snow and lead that came spattering down in rain.

It was through Nancy Sandars when I was still a student

Heythrop that I was led to take a more serious interest in prehistory. Nancy and Betty are two sisters who live alone together in the Manor House at Little Tew. Their garden is their lifework in a way or their life's calendar. It has a heaven-like profusion and simplicity. It is what Marvell's poetry would be like translated into reality. We had met through John Fuller, who I sometimes think is another modern projection of Marvell. Tew is the next village to Heythrop; we were usually free in the afternoon, so very often I walked over for tea. Their car was the most ancient, cared for like an invalid, their jam the best, their roses the most varied and sweet-smelling, their sitting-room the most crammed and fascinating, their soda-water machine the most wheezing, their typewriter the most eccentric I have ever known. They also had a few wonderful modern pictures, and they combined intellectual vigour and physical dash with the most restful and nourishing of England country appearance. I have seldom loved two people so much, or with such reason.

Nancy took the first shrewd step in my education by making me read *What Happened in History*, by Gordon Childe, who was the most talented and inspiring teacher of archaeology in the last generation. Of course nothing changes so fast and so often as the past, particularly when you have it safely organized in the store-rooms of museums and the pages of learned works. What Auden wrote is truer of archaeology than it is of politics.

> Our snipers sniping from the walls
> Of learned periodicals
> Our fact defend.
> Our intellectual marines
> Landing in little magazines
> Capture a trend.

But I was innocent of the furious quarrels, as I was of the newest techniques that were about to change and complicate archaeological method to a degree that puts the subject out of most people's reach. Gordon Childe writes with perfect lucidity, and so does Nancy Sandars in her *Prehistoric Art in Europe*, one of the few really great works of scholarship I have ever read when it was fresh. Gordon Childe's short book is not about written history; it interprets the evidences of archaeology. Nancy Sandar's book is not at all confined to art history; it deals with the whole outlook and the whole culture of prehistoric peoples. Yet if her work were confined to prehistoric art alone, this would still be the most important study of that subject. Archaeological lecturers have been heard to say there are no works of art, only artefacts, things made. That is upside-down language.

What I think happened is that early man had not distinguished art from its opposite. He whistled and sang like a bird, he chipped a blade of flint into the shape of an enormous laurel leaf. No one had told him not to do these things beautifully. Beauty was not a speciality; artists were not specialists. Certain objects were special, set aside, only because they were made over to the gods or to magic. As with things, so with actions. Rituals were not art, because there was no ritual which was non-art. I take it that we inherit almost everything we most value in one another, courage, love, vision, every instinct now called creative, from animals simpler than ourselves. But in the process of our long development, art has been more and more narrowed. A painter of coach panels was not an artist, nor at first was a printer. A painting on canvas was an artist's work, a canal barge was not. Once the canal barge-painter realized this, which happened rather recently, he stopped his despised work. Then it was understood that the painting of canal barges had been art after all. So then it was revived, not as part of barge-painting, but as part of 'art', with the stiff, unlovely and 'arty' results one can see. The same with 'art' bookbinding. How rightly someone said the other day that nothing is worse than the arts except the crafts.

It becomes clear enough from a study of prehistory, and even clearer if that is combined with a little reading in social anthropology, that no human societies are 'primitive' in the sense of being barbarous, uncultivated and gross because undeveloped, but many societies are decadent, their social form no longer performs its proper function. There have often been human societies that became perverted like rogue elephants. The appalling catastrophes of the so-called Dark Ages, which flung people after people out of Asia into the western extremities we now call Europe, mingling bloods and language everywhere and cementing the marriages by massacres, produced a map too complicated to draw, with a particular density of conflict and mobility of change at the far edge of Europe, in the last desirable islands, in Britain.

The independence of the southern Irish as we see it today is a temporary aberration, but it is also the last result of those convulsions which shook the world at the breakdown of the Roman empire in the west. The division is not racial. At one time the most crucial frontier in Europe, maybe in the world, between civilized, old-fashioned people and aggressive raiders, which meant between Christian and pagan, therefore between Romanized tribes of some kind and outsiders, ran through Eynsham and Woodstock. It was a frontier that shifted so constantly it can hardly be drawn, but you can still make out the small hillforts that once separated Wessex from Mercia. The division of Ireland is like that. But taken over longer time, Mercia was as fluid as a jelly-fish.

Another clear consequence of prehistory is that we all equally inherit blood guilt. No one has survived except as the offspring of murder and of massacre. Whether or not armed conflict is natural to mankind, which I greatly doubt, all of us have ancestors who shared in it, successful ancestors. We are the children of winners, of the ruthless and the blood soaked. The losers died young. The 1914 war, when the whole working population of Europe were commanded to murder one another, was the climax of a long and terrible process. Even inside the tiny cluster of the British islands purity of blood is unusual.

I wish I had known when I was taunted as a Jew by the Irish Brothers that the most traditional communities of all Ireland, the Arran islanders, are the offspring of Cromwellian soldiers. There are as few pure-blooded Jews as pure-blooded Irishmen. The old Garter King of Arms, a quiet, scholarly man whom I used to meet at lunch in a London club, used to amuse himself with a game he called sideways genealogy, in which you took two persons who seemed utterly distant, and then tried to relate them through common ancestors. He said he had never failed to do so within ten degrees of cousinage.

My Greek studies meandered in many directions, but their main current was double. In order to understand poetry I had strayed into art history and stumbled into archaeology and topography, and finally into the evidence for Greek popular religion. That led me to understand some kinds of intelligence and energy that are often dismissed as primitive. The keel of a wooden fishing boat is not primitive, nor is the sad and brilliant religion of Delphi. It was time to take another look at Stonehenge. In order to understand the poetry of Homer I had strayed into Anglo-Saxon, French, and many other medieval epic traditions, until at last I stumbled into Serbo-Croat, into pre-Islamic Arab poetry and the psalms of David. I thought I knew what values and what social conditions all this poetry had in common, and so I had the illusion of understanding Homer in a new way. I imagined a society in which one lived by honour. Once again, it was time to take a new look at the British equivalents. The most interesting characters in British history to me at that time were King Arthur and Robin Hood.

It was about 1966 that I learnt to ride a motorcycle. My ankles have never been strong enough since school to control the pedals of a car, so cars were no temptation. A tractor I could and did drive as a student; I used it to mow in a pleasant sloping field between woods and lake on early summer evenings. I was in charge of that wood, I loved it like a kingdom. I rebuilt its wooden gates, cleared its drains, restored an old vista, and came to know every bird in it. I learnt to ride the motorcycle at the age of thirty-five, hazardously, by following some younger man's advice to aim instead of steering. Nancy Sandars had been a formidable motorcyclist during the war, which somehow heartened me. She explained fast cornering by 'a sort of skating motion', which she made sound extremely stately. She was a motorcycle despatch rider.

The first motorcycle I had was a horrible little object, weak, slow, Japanese, and defective. Its gears slipped, its lights went out if you shook them, it had its work cut out to get up hills, and a bad wind blew it right across the road. But I took it to Avebury, to Stonehenge, and into London. Once a fly short-circuited it, several times it was stopped by deluges of rain, once it ran away from me at some traffic lights on a wet cobbled road and crashed to the ground roaring and panting, just at the feet of a policeman. On the longest of all its journeys, it brought me into a small town in Somerset terribly cold and wet after blowing into a ditch on a hilltop called Windy Corner, some kind of natural wind tunnel. I was told in the pub that anyone up there with a tractor made a fair income in winter, pulling out cars the wind blew over. My tiny motorcycle lasted through Dorset and Devonshire and the Somerset fens until I got to Dyrham, where the hill above the house was unexpectedly steep and we landed a little too fast in a great spurt of gravel within an inch of the Orangery windows.

Dyrham must I suppose dispute with Chatsworth the title of most beautiful grand house. The architect Talman worked at both, though neither house and certainly neither park depends entirely on his austere notions. Dyrham had always been a favourite of Tony Mitchell's. About this time he had just given up the wine trade, which the success and increasing business of his firm made intolerable to him. He had joined the National Trust, and Dyrham became his home and his headquarters. 'Don't talk to me about dry rot,' he said. 'I have forty chateaux with that, all falling down.' He was far busier than before, and I imagine less well off, but I think happy. He married a beautiful French girl he met at a grass conservation conference; she was an expert in the history of landscape gardens. It was as if one had known her a long time.

The reason for the steep hill under which Dyrham lies basking on summer days is that this, just as much as the hill above Broadway, is the scarp, the western edge of the Cotswolds. It was the battle of Dyrham in 577, when two Anglo-Saxon kings broke and killed three British kings, that opened up the whole valley of the Severn and the Welsh marches, and drove back the old people of the soil from that rich earth into the Black Mountains and beyond.

It seems likely enough that the Anglo-Saxons came streaming down the side of the Cotswolds where the British kings expected them. The number of kings on the British side adds a romantic streak to the story, but it suggests a whole society breaking up. I have heard it argued that the British in India, and therefore also the Romans in Britain, in imposing law by force, destroyed the growth of any authentic national unity; when they withdrew, they were responsible for the chaos they left. There is something in it, but before the Romans came the Celtic forests were already dark and heaving. I doubt whether pre-Roman Britain was a peaceful place, even though it may well have been happier, richer, more interesting, more humanly promising and more honourable, more virtuous.

Arthur is a pitiful relic on the whole. The site in Somerset called Camelot is just a field of grass that the sun makes glisten and the wind combs. You can see the mounds under the hedges. The wooded hill is English Arcadian. Once this was a little defended village with a fine wooden church; it even had a trading connection with Byzantium, a far more civilized and fruitful centre than Rome, where the Pope was not really adequate to do an Emperor's work. Nor of course was the Emperor, but Byzantine influence, at least in the arts, was more productive in Anglo-Saxon England even than in Rome at that time. I am not speaking of imports or imitations but of something new that was being born, and was born and then died. But the Anglo-Saxons of course were Arthur's enemies.

Arthur appears for the first time in a ninth-century Welsh history, and once in a Welsh proverb, that such a man was no Arthur. The discovery of his grave at Glastonbury was part of a medieval fund-raising campaign by that monastery. Arthur is less substantial than Robin Hood. He is only the sound of a trumpet far away, *triste, au fond des bois*.

One of the reasons why such dreadful things were done in these islands, why their conquest was a grim, uninterrupted, hacking war that took so long and repeated itself so often, is surely that the earth is rich and Britain is isolated. Not many invaders have coveted Iceland. Britain was almost equally remote. In civilized Byzantium almost the only two things that the most sophisticated historian knew of Britain were the legend of a romantic war over a princess, between the 'Angiloi' and a tribe beyond the Rhine, and the fact that the souls of the dead when they left their bodies sailed away in boats from Gaul into Britain. Into the west, he must have meant, into the sunset. Buzzing about the lanes on my motorcycle in that long green twilight which you get sometimes in a wet summer, I could see what he meant. It is still possible to get absurdly lost, and feel absurdly wrapped round by impenetrable hills, in western England.

There is a valley where I stayed once or twice with Bruce Chatwin, near Charles Tomlinson's austere poet's cottage. You more often meet a fox or a badger than a human being down there. It leads nowhere, it comes from nowhere. The valley floor is grass, but its walls are hanging woods dripping with dew and resounding with the voices of birds. The valley runs a long way, like a cleft in the rocks; no road leads into it, only a track. Near the valley head grows the remnant of a natural boxwood forest, more strange than beautiful. The trunks of the trees twist like ropes. Crawling through it is like dodging among greenish silver ropes entangled everywhere, behind the scenes of some petrified theatre. This valley lies below Wotton Under Edge. It is a long thin slice cutting into the wall of the Cotswolds. Maybe in places like that someone survived. But I doubt it. The Angles and the Saxons and the Germans and the Belgians covered this country like the slow seeping of water.

How isolated was England once, is a question like How dark were the Dark Ages? The darkness is in our eyes. If that is a measure of the ignorance, the simple-minded violence and confusion of the times, then we can say more certainly today, as historical science inches forward, that they were objectively quite dark and quite confused. When good King Alfred, to whose ambitious programme of translations into English we really owe the solid foundation of our written language, something that outlived many tribal languages of those days, came to geography, he added considerably to what the classical geography he translated already knew. Naturally he added most to northern Europe. But Alfred was a luminous and stunning exception. The fourteenth-century map of the world which is still to be seen in Hereford Cathedral has Northern Europe populated by such peoples as the one-legged men who lay on their backs in the shade of one enormous foot. Tacitus and Pliny make the same kind of suggestion, and so do the Norse sagas. Even in the sixteenth century maps were drawn showing 'Here be Dragons in the middle of Ireland'.

England was once part of a vanished world of which we know little today; in its folklore, in many of its traditions, and above all in its landscape, it still conveys that truth. One is always an outsider in England even to one's own traditions, let alone to those of the next village. The only secure inheritance is learnt by heart in childhood, it is not something learnt intellectually. It is a small, lighted area like a nursery, or so I have come to feel. If it were not for the work of the Opies on the language and lore of children, I would never have known that the rhymes my father taught me were different from those that other children knew. They come from a small Jewish area of east London where he spent a few years of childhood. He can only have picked them up in the street. Before the Vikings first raided Lindisfarne in 835 AD, the monks there, who were mostly Northumbrians, that is Angles, English, were already peacefully penetrated with Danish heroic poetry.

There is an important affinity, as I wrote in an earlier chapter, between the ideal of pagan or primitive heroism and that of the monks. God gave the law to Moses, says an Anglo-Saxon poem, and heroes and great warriors preserved it. In the *Orkney Saga* pagan heroism and Christian sanctity are hardly distinguishable. Alcuin of York rebuked the monks of Lindisfarne in 797 AD for their devotion to the Danish hero Ingeld. In the same way we owe all we have of ancient Irish heroic poetry and saga to the monks. *Beowulf* is a poem in English, made up in Mercia probably, for an English-speaking audience, with a continental hero and great Danish princes in it. How did the story, how did the poem travel? One wandering bard or generations of small poets in the small courts of country kings? The invisible strings that held that world together were epic poetry and heroic religion, a shared recognition of the obligation to blood vengeance, a shared respect for honourable death, which long outlived Christianity. Sometimes I think I have spent my whole life, with all its dispersed efforts, trying to understand 1914. The catastrophe to which history was leading happened in my father's lifetime.

I suppose I took my first idea of the obscurity of England, the idea that was so much refreshed by the tiny motorcycle in a wet summer, from the story of Alfred hiding in the Somerset fens. Day by day and year after year, whenever I went into the classics library, which is also the archaeological library at Oxford, inside the Ashmolean Museum, I brooded over the Alfred jewel. Denis thought of writing a thesis once on Anglo-Saxon jewellery. The Alfred jewel embodies a central paradox of that age, being so delicate as it is, so mannered, and yet so confident, in a certain sense so barbaric. The bold English lettering and the brilliant, strange colouring of it do not seem to have come out of any fen: and yet still less from any great metropolitan centre. Not that Alfred's world was intellectually unambitious. They say the jewel was part of a pointer for reading, probably a present sent to a bishop with the new translation of Gregory on the duty of bishops, the flagship of Alfred's great fleet of translations. If I have mentioned this jewel more than once, that is because I have stopped to look at it at least once a month, sometimes much more often, for more than thirty years. Many things have moved on and altered position around it, even the library door has moved round a corner, but Alfred's jewel is still rooted to the spot.

Perhaps one ought to say more about the love of objects and the contents of museums. My own passion for them is unashamed, although I am not a collector. Things pile up in my possession by mistake, like a sort of humus, books being the worst offenders, but sometimes one shakes oneself like an elderly mountain, and a landslide of untidiness disappears. I do not see how you can have any deep interest in human beings or in their history, in their development, without admitting to learn from things made. Whether you will learn more from a vast fortified settlement like Maiden Castle or from the little harp in the Sutton Hoo treasure depends entirely on how you set about it, the quality of your brooding, what books you read. The first certainty is that only arrogance and silly prejudice confine any scholar to a library. It was not only a nice symbol but a useful arrangement in my young days that both the British Library and the Ashmolean Library were in the middle of museums. In both places you could come out and wash your dizzy eyes by resting them on physical things. Things seldom offer reliable solutions, but they do generate excellent questions. This problem reminds me of Doctor W. G. Grace, who never read print in the season, as it spoiled his eye for the ball.

It was the technical procedures of archaeology that held me at a distance for so long. After a few stray lectures and some old-fashioned books I developed paranoia about flints, above all the minute ones called microliths, and about beakers and 'beaker folk'. Peoples were always called folk by early archaeologists; in nineteenth-century pages they constantly indulge in what the Germans taught us to call folk-wanderings. One wave of invasion of this country used to be traced, perhaps it still is, as a slow progression across Salisbury Plain, through the odd habit of opening an ancient grave-mound every so many years and every so many miles, and popping in a few more dead men with easily datable equipment. The worst kind of archaeological lecture used to be medieval. It consisted entirely of pacings and of ground plans. Sometimes the pacing itself had been done in the Middle Ages and the building had vanished, which gave at least a ghostly charm to the proceedings.

The truth is that archaeology is not quite a science, not quite an art, and only an insubordinate daughter of history. Least of all is it a body of knowledge. It can be learned only through experience and through practice. It draws on many sciences. It is a technique, or a set of techniques, as surgery is. In our lifetimes the techniques have already been rapidly refined, and in some directions possibly over-specialized. The grand scale excavation of great sites that flourished before the war is impossible now; that has advantages for accuracy and thoroughness, but it has some disadvantages as well. One can admit also that treasure-hunting is a wasteful, destructive and gross procedure, without turning up one's nose at treasures and calling them artefacts. They were made as treasures, hoarded as treasures and often buried as treasures. They are sometimes worth every penny of the millions they fetch at Sotheby's. Today we look like spending a generation pecking like hens at the dust, but it is not possible even in principle, and God knows it is not desirable, to exhaust the possibilities of describing any natural object, even the dust. When we read the dust of any site of human habitation as fully and scientifically as brother human beings can bear to do, the tale it tells is painful, even appalling, but that is what we seek to record. It is What happened in history? or What is a human being? We must go a long, roundabout route to find out that.

Man is the proper study of mankind, but the experience of

different ages and lifetimes alters that study greatly. Archaeology and Christianity and literature do not throw an equal light. For me, each of the three always led back into the others. I ought to make it clear that my position as a priest was peculiar. I had no parish work unless I sought it out, I seldom administered the Christian sacraments, few of my private friends were believers, my studies were not theological, and my journeys were seldom missionary journeys. But I believed perfectly in everything I did and said: I gave public sermons and often spoke about religion. What I believed then I believe now. The difference between my religion and a layman's was only in the intensity of meditation, in the time spent on serious thought. Archaeology entered as intimately into the way I considered mankind as Greek and Hebrew enter into Christian theology. History, particularly the sadness of history, entered my thoughts at least as deeply as the daily experience of a Christian priest.

I will record some of the ways in which one subject seemed to lead back into another, and to grow deeper, during my first ten years teaching at Oxford, from 1965 to 1975, between my thirty-fourth and my forty-fourth birthday. When I left Heythrop as a priest in 1964 I had hardly begun to scrape the surface of real archaeology. That year, I lived at Tremeirchion, under an old Jesuit guru, the kindest taskmaster I have ever known, a sort of saintly Leo McKern. We were there to make our souls, only for life in this world not in the other. For some people the experience hastened and for others retarded natural and moral processes, rather as the weather affects an apple. I spent a lot of time exploring Welsh hillforts. It was orthodox to say these places were not linked, but there were so many in a row, on the edge of the hills, that I could hardly believe that. They looked to me not like forts but like villages. Several of them were scarcely excavated at that time, and only a thorough excavation can answer the questions any fool can ask.

But it has recently been shown that even at Cranbury Chase, where Pitt-Rivers, the founding methodical genius of British archaeology, discovered a fortress of refuge, his technique was too crude to notice the post-holes of a wooden village, or the ancient field system which is still visible outside the barricades. Pitt-Rivers was an old soldier who spoke of *redans*. He first learnt his method by classifying the muskets and early rifles in the Tower of London. How odd that those grim walls should have given us British watercolour painting through Paul and Thomas Sandby and modern archaeology through Colonel Lane-Fox. He altered his name to Pitt-Rivers when he inherited land (and what land!) in Dorset, and started digging. His mobile headquarters was a shepherd's hut on wheels, a kind of caravan, which is still I think in use in an Oxford car park, where a married student of archaeology lives in it. Pitt-Rivers had an influence and a prestige that are hard to measure. Archaeology now is beginning to reveal more about the arts of peace and less about the architecture of war. All the same, both exist, they existed in combination, and one led almost inevitably to the other. The meaning of heroic poetry is to call this tragic and by irony to call it destiny.

Nonetheless what was done is shocking, and it taught the English to behave worse. I have said nothing about crusades or civil war, the barons' wars or any others, but the generations of armoured dinosaurs chopping one another to pieces that were finally blasted away only by gunpowder and monarchic sovereignty, the absolute state, continued the same story; the futile rebellions of peasants hacking their masters to bits with billhooks, just as they shot down the tin soldiers of French chivalry with wooden arrows, merge into the sullen mood that Thomas More repressed as Protestantism: he feared it as a revival of Lollardy, just another upheaval of the crazy peasants against the throne.

The same generation that were thrilled at Cambridge by the classics and by paganism in the time of Christopher Marlowe will have survived, if they lived to be old, long enough to see the King's head sliced off at Whitehall. But it is not these civil wars and profound disturbances that I mean by behaving worse. It is the almost casual violence and horror of tortures and executions and the treatment of slaves. One cannot say they were treated worse than animals, because animals were also treated badly. The common pets of the sixteenth century were slobbering great carnivorous hounds and head-tearing hawks. It is one of the miracles of history that the poet of that age was Shakespeare and not Ted Hughes. Indeed it is a lesson worth pondering.

Homer's compassion is ironic and stoical; what we call tragedy is an intonation of Homeric narrative, a momentum that was already present when these verses were chanted with equal stress. The compassion is infinite, almost post-Christian, by comparison with the hard tragical quality of Anglo-Saxon doom.

> It is the soft clashing of claymores you hear
> That they carry to the house.
> Hoar wolf's howl, hard wood-talk,
> Shield's answer to shaft.

For me studying the ancient Greeks was like being perpetually in the company of soft-eyed, brilliant children. An illusion, of course. As the proverb goes, they were as clever as a barrel full of monkeys. The deeper I sank into ancient Greek writings, the sadder and more blood-encrusted by comparison the Dark Ages of my own country seemed. Between the time of Stonehenge and the time of Shakespeare, one could hardly fail to think the Greeks superior in most things, even in the quality of their suffering. But as time went on the two peoples drew together in my thoughts, partly through modern history, through the likeness and unlikeness of Greeks and British as allies in the last war, and partly through the objective insight that the world, or at least Europe, had become one place archaeologically long before the Romans were first seasick in the Channel.

Classical Greece was an area of bright lamplight that we know through written language, but lamplight supposes a surrounding darkness which defines it, and one can discover a great deal about the lighted area by probing the darkness. I have written elsewhere about the class division of landowners who hunt and whose weapons are glorious or ornamental, as against a simple, more or less stable peasantry not unlike serfs, a division that was in working order all over Europe until this present century, and can be traced back archaeologically to the time of the Myceneans, in places as far apart as Brittany and the Crimea. It was in common between the so-called light and the so-called darkness. If we had the lost heroic poetry of pre-Roman Gaul, as we have its spectacular treasures of metalwork, we might revise our opinions of the dark area. In the middle and late sixties, I was trying to fit the darkness together like a jigsaw puzzle.

Most of life after all has usually been the slow grazing of cattle and the spinning of cloth. The country people of many generations have had the same preoccupations. No change of politics or religion alters that very much. Sometimes places that flourished for a time in antiquity have gone back to what they were before they flourished, and now we think ourselves skilful to trace their ramparts and pick over their ruins. Archaeological knowledge does not always follow historical importance. Ancient places are not all equally known. For example Crickley Hill above Gloucester and the Severn plain, which was so romantic to Ivor Gurney, has now been thoroughly excavated. Indeed, until the last few years there was no hillfort we knew quite so much about. Yet about Mont Lassois, given its obvious importance, we know rather little. I first arrived there on a pilgrimage through the heart of France, on the old Route Nationale from Geneva to Calais. Mont Lassois is a bristling, hog-backed hill in a crook of the upper Seine, at a point where the Seine is no bigger than the Thames at Lechlade, but very much quieter and more unexploited. It looks like just another little fishing river. But in the connection of barbarian Europe, even of the British islands, with Greece, this is the most important place in the world.

Just south of Mont Lassois lies a much more serious hill, which pours out within a few miles of each other the source of the Seine and the source of the Irigoine. The Seine is a Victorian, or in this case Second Empire shrine of pilgrimage, with the spring in a cave and a ridiculous marble nymph, set among huge and dismal coniferous trees. The Irigoine is a strong little wild trickle, quite lost on a hillside in the woods. But the Irigoine flows into the Rhone and reaches the Mediterranean, the sea that washes Italy and Greece. So it is not so surprising as it might be that Mont Lassois was in contact with the Greeks in the sixth and early fifth centuries BC. On the southern end of the hogback of Mont Lassois stands a small church with a cemetery that belongs to the old village of Vix. In a funeral mound, I suppose one of those tumps like big grass-grown molehills which are still to be seen if one follows the river, the Vix treasure was found. The mound was the fifth-century burial of a Gaulish princess, with a magnificent wooden cart, of which the bronze hubs look as if they were made yesterday, some Greek and some Etruscan fine pottery, golden ornaments, and a great, dark bronze wine-mixer, its body beaten bronze and its heavy ornaments finely-moulded bronze, six feet high and of Spartan workmanship.

Apart from things one can see in the city of Athens and in the British Museum, no Greek object has ever been found to compare with this. It is a thing of stunning beauty and intricate design, but of far more strength than beauty. One must see it in its home, in the small local museum at the top of some tower stairs in Chatillon sur Seine, to conceive of its impressive scale. It poses the unanswered question of how on earth it ever got to Mont Lassois. Its body in places is only one millimetre thick, yet it gives the impression of great weight. It could not have come all the way by water. Was it resold from Marseilles, or commissioned from a Spartan workman in south Italy, to seal a treaty or to celebrate a marriage? The Greeks offered presents of this grandeur only to the gods. In fact Croesus, King of Lydia, offered enormous wine-mixers to Apollo at Delphi, but his were made of gold. Can this giant piece of bronze have been looted from a sanctuary? But there are plenty of other Greek bits and pieces from Mont Lassois, which indicate friendly relations. No doubt an excavation will tell us much more one day. As a peace offering to the masters of a trade route, this awkward and heavy work of art would be an exaggerated gift.

It makes one rub one's eyes with incredulity. The Greek influence on Britain is almost all indirect. It hardly amounts to very much. In idle hours I imagine a Greek burial in Cornwall or the Isle of Wight, even a ship of the sixth or fifth century BC carried as far north as the Scottish islands. All we have is a solid ship's anchor like the blade of a giant's pickaxe, which came out of the sea off Anglesey. It was made in Alexandria before the Romans got here, but who knows what ship went down with it? On the mainland opposite Skye we have two mysterious stone towers built against raiders of some kind, at just the time the Romans invaded Britain. Had they sent a reconnaissance mission so far north? That is not impossible; a little while later two Roman centurions reached Uganda by taking a canoe up the Nile. But the majority of the evidence that ties Britain to Greek Europe is humbler and less romantic. It is the tin trade and the amber trade, a scattering of Greek coins in the south, or at an earlier time the sudden appearance in the north of new techniques of carpentry, new and sharp tools for boat-making. They were used for sewing together the planks of wooden boats.

I first saw the museum at Chatillon sur Seine with John Berger, who had once stumbled on it by chance. What impressed him first was the surrealist quaility of the bronze like a railway engine in a bedroom. Later I saw it again with a string of different friends, in fact with anyone who was willing to take me there. I first heard of Vix at an Oxford evening lecture, where an elderly professor like an enraged bantam cock berated the lecturer for missing the purpose of this enormous work of art. The professor had, I thought at the time, drunk a bottle or two, but on reflection I am less sure. His excitement was purely intellectual. Had we not in Greek the account of a strange and barbarous manner in which a people presumed to be Celtic discovered the future? They murdered a human being, and estimated the oracle's reply by noting how the blood spurted into a pot. Was this not just such a pot? A more modest professor further back cleared his throat and stuttered. In that case, he asked, why was it fitted with a perforated metal wine-strainer?

The trouble with my visits to Chatillon was that we were always in a hurry. We always stopped for lunch at the Café de l'Europe, the one with the photograph of young wild pigs on the bedroom staircase. Around Mont Lassois, the *sanglier* is on his home ground. But after the museum and after lunch, there was never the necessary day to explore the hill itself. I did so in the end, for the first time, not many years ago. It was Easter, and the fields were very green and sprinkled with fresh long-legged cowslips. The hill of Mont Lassois turned out to be badly overgrown and more informative from a distance than it was close up. At the far end, the northern, downstream end of the hogback, one could easily make out the lines of ramparts and gate-towers, grass-grown heavings of the soil. Not far away there were isolated graves. It snowed out of a clear sky. We should have known, because the air was sharp, it smelt of snow. In a village café where we took refuge, a farmer told us how he had plagued the archaeologists for years until they dug out the treasure of Vix. There was a clang, he said, whenever he ploughed round it. Can that be true? Certainly the published photograph of this famous excavation looks like some Scotland Yard detectives in an Ealing comedy inspecting a flooded bomb crater, or a dozen Watsons crowding round the grave of Sherlock Holmes.

I have written elsewhere that because this huge piece of bronze would be so difficult to move, it may not have been the bronze, but a maker, perhaps a slave, who was brought to Mont Lassois. If Greek masterpieces were made in Italy, why not in France among the wild boars? The bronze workmanship of the Gauls at that time was at least equally impressive, as I already knew from Nancy Sandars, and as one can see at Chatillon, just by observing the wheel-hubs of the funeral cart. But I think now that whoever made this masterpiece had a whole experienced workshop to help him, and it was staffed with Greeks. This is a question of delicacy and precision, and of the perfect control of proportions. The great vessel is not, as I used to think, a magnified version of a not uncommon shape of pot, given to the gods as poor men gave miniature versions, but always in the same proportions. This piece was designed to give just the effect it does give: it is awe-inspiring. Its proportions are cunningly varied like those of the Parthenon, to impress our eyes. It travelled by cart I suppose, wrapped in straw. Sailing right up the Rhone was not easy in those days, any more than it is now.

The question of slavery ought to be considered in the context of the forest rides or tracks that such a cart must have travelled. Caesar used them in his day, though they were not the broad, straight military highways of the late Roman Empire, always symbolically going nowhere. Roman roads were clearly intended for rushing about to meet imminent disaster, just as the great crumbling ornamental gateways of cities in the Libyan sands seem positively intended for the arrival of bad news. One of the saddest things about the Norman invasion of England is the thought of Harold's exhausted army storming southward along Roman roads still passable after six hundred years, from the Norse invasion at Stamford Bridge to the low slope of hill where they stood their ground not far from the Channel coast. Both the Normans and the Norsemen had some claim to England, by the dynastic and feudal arguments of the time. If ever there was a doomed people it was the Anglo-Saxons.

Slavery and fear stopped the forest roads. What the Greeks had already done to the Sicilians in the fifth century BC, the Romans did later to Gaul and to Britain. As the Greeks got richer, and the Romans richer still, the whole world around them was troubled. First they traded, then they adventured, then they colonized and slaughtered and enslaved. That is the whole early history of Europe. The famous patch of light created the darkness, I believe. The Romans caused a chaos of despairing tribal wars and heroic migrations as far off as the borders of China and the Vistula; and the resulting tidal wave of aggression is what overwhelmed them in the end. For five hundred years under the Romans all Britain was a slave farm, where conditions steadily got worse.

For another five hundred years, wave after wave of invaders hacked one another to pieces. From 1066 onwards, the Normans got to work on the Scots and the Irish and the Welsh, while they kept the screws on the native English; they lasted another five hundred years. Shakespeare's Caliban is the parody of an Irishman, as his name and his song imply. From the sixteenth century on, the British treated every native people in the world they could get at in much the way they had learnt to treat each other. The natives of North America and Australia were massacred in the full light of the nineteenth century. It was a successful method, and it lasted nearly four hundred years. Does anyone think that the trouble in Belfast can simply be reasoned away? Perhaps it can in the end; I believe so, but that is part of believing in the human race. We who do so have a lot of evidence against us.

CHAPTER EIGHT

The Shadow of the Trees

> They will take away the shadow of the trees, they will take it
> they will take from you the shadow of the sea, they will take it
> they will take away the shadow of the heart, they will take it
> they will take away your shadow.
>
> George Seferis

LIVING A LIFE, as the Russians say, is not just taking a walk across a field. The ten years or more that I worked at Greek archaeology were not untroubled. I led a strange life for a priest, and a bizarre life for a scholar. By spending so long in Greece, in a prolonged love affair with that country that was not exclusively scholarly, I came to see at close quarters the result of seven years of dictatorship. That made one think a good deal. It did not increase one's respect for established order in church or state, though it made me grateful for English policemen and cups of tea. I even became a royalist again, though only in this country and in Russia, and always with the condition that I am glad the Duke of Edinburgh is not an absolute monarch. But it was unsatisfying to be so much abroad, so much in Oxford, so much wandering about doing clerical odd-jobs. Archaeology demands a dedication, scholarship a concentration; priesthood demands both, it absorbs time more and more absolutely as one grows older. It also requires quite good health, or at least a certain sturdiness of disposition. By 1974, as a priest I was falling to pieces.

The most interesting lesson about priesthood that I learnt from life was one I learnt early; I mean the limits of what one individual in this world can do to help another. That applies to priest, doctor, schoolmaster and all lovers of mankind. There are really people you cannot help at all; you cannot cure them, or make them morally better, or teach them, or make them happy. To have any illusions about this is to be like the clergyman in *The Way of all Flesh*, happy when an old suffering woman loses consciousness because she is 'safe in the arms of Jesus'. Neither life nor death is safe, and almost everything that consoles us is false. It is the right and in a way the dignity of every human being to defy cure or comfort, though that is a sad dignity, and most people can be helped in one way or another. They can even be educated, even cured of a deep wound. But one should give only what people need or want, and in the way they need or want it. In the same way one must accept the blackest truth about human history, without pretending things were less bad. It is a bad fault and not an unusual one to insist on curing or reforming or comforting, and then to lose patience, to blame the wicked client, when this process, this illusion one had of one's efficacy, is rejected.

From an early interest in rebellious children, and then in absolutely destitute men unable to be transformed by any social worker, priest or prison officer, I came to like working in prisons. I was a relief chaplain employed for a few days or a few weeks. The work was terribly demanding, and I do not think I could have stood it physically for as long as a year, although to leave the prison for a life in the sunnier and grassier quadrangles of Oxford, and to abandon those grim, friendly faces for a gentle nibble at scholarly periodicals, left one feeling uneasy. Perhaps if I had done a prison job permanently, I might have worked out a way of combining activities, but I know no one who has done so. When prison chaplains get away, they switch off and try to recharge themselves by gardening or by fishing in rivers. I survived only as a substitute. Nowadays all Catholic chaplains need positive security clearance, because of the IRA, but I was sworn in so long ago that the process was simple. Like everyone else who works inside a prison, I signed the Official Secrets Act, and that was that.

Therefore one can say little about what happened. But for the purpose of this book I need only one or two general truths. Prison is like school, an inferior boarding school. The food is frankly awful, though the men seem to mind it less than I would. It smells of custard and gravy as school food used to smell. I always imagined bread and water as a Shakespearean penance with which one might be content. Today it would be Thames tap water in a plastic cup, and pre-sliced rubber bread. The warders are as nice and as nasty as average schoolmasters. The governors are just like headmasters, they vary in the same way. Non-communication of every kind takes place.

As I was working in Brixton, which was then the remand prison for the whole London area, I had an enormous, very varied flock. Whatever happens in the world of crime happens first in London. The place was overcrowded, to put it mildly, and contained many subnormal or extremely inadequate men who ought to have been in hospitals. But Brixton was governed at that time with some subtlety and humanity. The prison officers won my sincere respect. Their private sense of justice was rough, but their behaviour on the whole was extremely correct. They would do anything for the men in their care if they felt they could do the least good.

Of course they were cynical about criminals. Chaplains are supposed to be soft-shelled and soft-boiled, so I was often prodded by the prison officers to see whether the men were taking me for any rides. I adopted the truthful answer that I had nothing against most of the men, I liked some of them greatly, the only trouble with them was that most of them ought to be in prison. This answer was acceptable, but it was easy to see that the officers greatly respected any special effort one made on behalf of any of the men. Just so long as one spoke without moral optimism. I am afraid they were right too, much more often than not. I came to believe there really is a criminal class. Its distinguishing mark is stupidity, they are less intelligent than most people. But at the same time they have greater cunning, and an immoral tendency to take short cuts at other people's expense. They foolishly thought they would get away with something. They have more vanity and envy and self-pity than most people, a worse chip on their shoulder. Of course these things are not true of everyone who goes to prison, but I thought they were true of the majority of convicted prisoners. I have almost never met a wicked man, though I did once, and in prison I almost never observed a moral reformation, an inner change, though there were exceptions even to that. Several times I saw innocent men embittered. Any system more useless and dead-headed and ill-considered than the present English prison system I would not like to encounter.

The oddest part of my job was to have charge of Provo and IRA prisoners, most of whom were formally and a handful actually Catholics. Not unnaturally, most of the prison officers took a poor view of these men, and wondered greatly what a chaplain would find to say to them. One is never supposed to discuss a man's case with him as a priest, although in fact the case often overlaps with what one must discuss. One is certainly not supposed to discuss politics when preaching to the IRA. One's job is to maintain a relation of confidence, in order to give them what religious help they need or ask for. It is like offering a cigarette to a dying man, and it is something from home. Thank heaven for the universality and objectivity of Catholic services. Some of these Irish prisoners were rough and passionate political extremists, whose equivalent you might meet in any European country. Those who distressed me most were hardly more than schoolboys. They were not wicked or violent or mad or stupid. They had just made an error of moral calculus, which they could now see for themselves without any instruction from me. They regretted their mistake. Their relationship to murder was freakish. They were polite, well-spoken, and very, very young. They were like boys I was at school with, they were what one might have been. They had been used. One boy was tried at seventeen for a crime committed at fifteen: that of taking a parcel bomb to the post.

A lot of Irish prisoners thought they were going to be

amnestied. It is always terrible to speak to a man beginning a very long sentence, but that illusion made things worse. It is not the chaplain's duty to drive any man to despair. IRA prisoners young or old were always shocked and saddened by the attitude of other prisoners. They had imagined through God knows what twist of their fantastical theory that they were the allies of the British working class. The other long-term prisoners left them in no doubt about their mistake. I have no way of knowing how deep their sadness went, but I do think half of them were ashamed. I often wondered from a few cases I came across whether IRA membership was transmitted by inheritance, through women; it was seldom a case of father and son. When the men saw their families I often had to be present. I remember a conversation with an aunt that worried me because it seemed both perky and in some way artificial. If any illegal message was being passed, I was responsible. At the same time there were two children present and it was my deep responsibility to try to make the visit go as well it could. Later that afternoon I had to rush outside the prison gates, having forgotten to give the aunt a phone number she wanted. She was a different woman, stricken, broken to pieces, with tears streaming down her face.

I was forty-five years old. That was the terribly hot summer when the elm disease had ravaged England, but dead elm trees were still standing up like giant skeletons in every hedge. The sky was bluer than anyone remembered it, the sun was blazing. The prisoners sunbathed in their tarmac yards. They mounted a strike against prison conditions, refusing to move indoors. The governor left them in their yard until they tired of it. It was too hot to do anything else. Those clanging iron staircases wore the soles off my shoes and the skin off my feet. Having learnt the art of liking people in place of the theology of loving them, I was enjoying myself; prisoners after all are pleased to see one and grateful for the least benefit. In the fields outside London a new shape of baled straw was beginning to appear. Instead of the Stonehenges and the Hoar Stones of straw in great rectangular blocks, some new machine was leaving them in long cylinders like rolled up bedding. The heat and the drought were affecting the beech trees; they were beginning to die in their turn. Someone told me every mature beech tree has to drink two hundred gallons a week from underground. Can that be true?

That autumn I was hanging on by a thread to my old vocation and my complicated way of life. The next spring I left the Jesuits and got married, having been more and more in love for something like thirteen years. *Et nos cedamus amori.* The inward history, the infancy and youth of love, and the disturbance I had felt are not part of this book. They have been charted in poems. It is enough to say that the love of one person had at last become my everything. So I resigned. At once, my life was utterly transfigured. Campion Hall was suddenly as distant as the mountains of the moon. Private life with someone you love is the greatest of human pleasures. My old life washed away nearly at once, with the sour blessing of a Roman court. At first I could hardly realize how free I was, and I hesitated to begin life over again.

I tried for a number of jobs, with more spiritedness than hope of success, but I clung for five more years to teaching the classics. For three years I used a room at Christ Church that gazed across Tom Quad from high up under the tower. But in the end I settled down at home to write. A piece of blank paper is the only thing in the world I have a serious ambition to control. My own college of St Catherine's is like enough to home, far more so than the bird's nest in Christ Church. Or being in St Catherine's is like being in 'a wood near Athens'. My studies there have a freshness that was lacking.

Where we live now, you can see Wichwood from the upper windows. Stonesfield is a quarrying village where the quarrying stopped. It has some fine cottages, an early thirteenth-century church, and a big old rectory now renamed Manor House. Ours is the oldest cottage, with a long green garden under the churchyard wall, and an antique pear tree under the windows which fills up with blossom as white as paper and small red pears as hard as bullets.

We chose our cottage on the first day we saw it; we walked to the far end of the garden, which was a wilderness then that I thought untamable, but as we looked back at the house the sun suddenly came out and all the church bells sounded; the pear tree was in full blossom. It would have been hard to resist. Having settled, we soon found cats on the wall, one of whom adopted us and constantly sits on this paper as I try to write. We bought a small dog that fell deeply in love with the car. He thinks the car is an animal and kisses it when it comes home. The cat lies for hours on the car roof, sleeping or watching the swifts that breed in the woodshed and gather on the telephone wires. An ordinary village house that was once a smallholding.

This is not the countryside as I used to imagine it. The big bones of Lancashire and Yorkshire set a standard we can hardly live up to. The downs have a beauty and concordant rhythm as if the earth had been transfigured there. 'And did those feet in ancient time?' always reminds me of the downs near Lewes. Around Stonesfield there are certain places and certain views that grow into you without your ever stopping to stare. They constantly catch your eye, as they vary quietly on from season to season. I hope all this is not a metaphor for death; sages have often noticed that quality in peaceful countryside. I think the continuity and the touches of handsomeness, even the few moments of real beauty, are all a metaphor for a deeper kind of life than most of us have come to expect. The landscape close to Oxford still has a few gleams and glimpses, but it gets scruffier every year. It is scabbed with assertions; envy has infected it like mildew. Come out of her, O my people.

So living where the ground heaves itself up so gently and the oldest roads are like the opening of the sea for the children of Israel, we began to explore the countryside. I began to snuffle like an antiquarian shooting dog. The Roman road is the village boundary. On an early autumn Sunday you can bring home thirty or forty kinds of flowering weeds. The woods are a green larder, with wild strawberries and wild gooseberries, and herbs of every kind. Cowslips still grow on the hillside fields in more profusion than stars in the summer sky. Even in childhood I never saw so many. Nor so many violets as grow along one or two field hedges in this village. A week or two ago we counted three dozen butterflies in four or five gardens, in the ivy and on ragged clumps of asters. In the winter it snows, the roads are always cut for a few days, the wind blows steadily and severely out of the north. Bread and milk come in by tractor.

England is nothing but a place, really. But what hidden, unassertive goodness of the earth, and what memories in the stones. I have always been repelled from the admittedly overwhelming interest of Homeric archaeology, because what the scholars find and dispute over throws so little light on Homer; Homer is a book. In the same way I have always neglected biblical archaeology, enthralling as that is, because what lights up the Bible best is the inward meaning of its own pages. Now I think the countryside is a book. You must read it in its own terms, and that will take you many years for a few poor miles of ground. I hope this does not sound like a mystical or an anti-scientific idea. I still read the Homeric and the biblical archaeologists, and we are all of us made conscious nowadays of the many different sciences that go to explain one bit of simple landscape. We are none of us masters of them all, we can only scrape about. The botany, the history, the geology, the study of behaviour in plants and animals, the archaeology, the painter's eye, and for all I know the astrophysics that hang around the head of our sleeping village, like cloud on cloud, would exhaust more than one lifetime. That is to leave out theology, architecture, gardening, forestry, fruit, weather, and the breeding history of cattle.

Around Stonesfield, a number of simple mysteries remain. I think I know why the violets favour the north side of their hedge, but what and precisely where is Allen's grave? It is easy to spot on a large scale map; it was clearly a boundary landmark, and so a landmark of disputed ground, just beyond the Roman road. But the story that belonged to it was lost a long time ago, and now I think the place is lost. The boundaries of Stonesfield make sense, one can see in every direction how they happened. Under the village runs the river Evenlode, and beyond that the railway from Oxford to Hereford. Beyond that again lies one of the last tentacles of Wichwood. The first really preoccupying problem I had about this landscape arose from the old thrill of mounds and tumps, but it led to the same bleak understanding of our history I have expressed in other chapters. The problem began with trying to trace on an Ordnance Survey map a vallum of dyke, an earth rampart with a ditch, that has left a grotesquely long trail all over this district. Grim's Dyke is its name.

Grim is the devil of the Anglo-Saxons, so the ditch was prehistoric in their time, like the ruins of the city of Bath.

> Snapped rooftrees, towers fallen,
> the work of the Giants, the stonesmiths,
> mouldereth.
> Rime scoureth gatetowers
> rime on mortar.

The Grim's Dyke that swoops in a great circle around Stonesfield is not a stone ruin, only an earthwork. Indeed it seems that the devil bulldozed or scooped out all the earthworks of Britain, but the giants of ancient times built the stone cities that the Saxons found in ruins. The Greeks in a similar situation spoke of the architecture of the ancient Cyclopes, meaning stones no living man could lift: the walls of Mycenae for instance. They spoke also of stones brought together by magic, by flute music. Was that because wandering masons measured the foot unit by the length of an octave between stops on the flute they carried? That is what happened at the building of Chartres, I believe. Or only because a flute called out time like a work song, like a drumbeat to the galley

slaves? The Saxons were a rougher and a more frightene
people. Only the devil had the strength to plough so deep an
so uselessly. They understood strength. The devil and hi
works were familiar to them; they named farms and village
after the devil.

There are Grimthorpes and Grim's Dykes all over England
At Grimsbury Castle in Berkshire he has a bottomless pond n
man can measure, with a golden calf drowned in it. I
nineteenth-century Greece that would have been twelv
golden pigs with twelve golden piglets, or seven golden duck
with seven golden ducklings, but the golden calf is biblical
suppose and more sinister. At the other end of Oxfordshir
from us, the devil ploughed the whole of Grim's Bank in on
night. The ditch and the rampart are his furrow, the roun
borrows are the scrapings of his ploughshare, and the smal
mound is a huge clod of earth he flung at his imp for no
ploughing the whole affair straight. Maybe after all they wer
not so frightened of the devil as one might think. Maybe yo
get to black humour about Grim as you begin to lose belief i
him. Anyway, Stonesfield lies between the small river Evenlod
and the two huge estates of Blenheim and Ditchley with thei
woods full of pheasants and their outlying farms. Blenheim o
course is a recent name, but Ditchley is an old wasteland,
piece of hunting forest named after Grim's Dyke which run
through it from end to end.

The endless, sluggish extent of this rampart was not notice
or fully plotted until O. G. S. Crawford traced it in 1930, an
published it in an early issue of his magazine *Antiquity*. At tha
time, Crawford was fresh from the triumph of his pioneerin
survey, *Wessex from the Air*. In fact he had more or les
invented that subject. He produced no air photographs o
Grim's Dyke, and maybe he took none, but he did survey it
whole length both on foot and from the air. That was the yea
before I was born. The survey on foot would have been easie
and the aerial survey cheaper in those days. Much less of th
dyke survives today, and walking is more restricted. What i

worse, the specialized excavations that have taken place here and there along its length have piled up more doubts than findings. It really is problematic. Crawford's argument is still formidable. He traced something like thirty-five miles of more or less continuous ramparts, enclosing some twenty square miles of ground.

They run across the parklands of Blenheim, snake their way through Ditchley, disappear inside Cornbury Park on the edge of Charlbury, and reappear on the far side of the river Evenlode, crossing Ramsden Heath and circling back towards Long Hanborough. The only unexplained missing section of Crawford's reconstruction is easily supplied by the line of the river Glyme, between Stratford Bridge near Wootton, a small road-bridge where I once saw a wet-coated animal in the reeds with long front teeth like a beaver, and the spot near Bladon where the Glyme meets the Evenlode. What was once the modest Glyme for most of that distance is now Blenheim lakes. Where Capability Brown has been at work, no mere excavation will recover much trace of the past. Every surviving twist of those tiny rivers, every rotting willow stump full of flowers is written into the rags of my soul, but what good is that to an archaeologist? Archaeology, as we said, is a technique like surgery, at its worst like dental surgery, but love is not.

We are talking about a big area of land. It includes at least six known Roman villas and their land, most of Blenheim, most of Ditchley, and much of Cornbury, which is another huge estate, nowadays the most private of the three. To put it another way, the rampart encloses a long stretch of the Evenlode valley, four or five separate modern villages, and some varied country, including hills and valleys, heath, forest, stone quarries, and river meadows that flood in winter. There is no one spot from which you see quite all of this extent. Akeman Street, the Roman military road that runs the whole way from Cirencester to St Albans, cuts right across the middle of Grim's Dyke. If this area had a centre, then the modern village of Stonesfield must be close to the spot. But nothing left standing here is older than 1200 AD or as old: not one cottage and not one tree and not one stone of the church. The hill path down to the river is a quarry path. The people were smallholders like Scottish crofters; they dug the famous Stonesfield roof tiles, which you find all over the Cotswolds, out of mines in the ground, and let them stand all winter for the frost to split them naturally. That industry may be very old indeed, certainly as old as the Romans. But it hardly explains thirty-five miles of ramparts.

Out in the fields towards Blenheim, hardly a quarter of a mile from the Roman road and only a foot or so under the prosperous crops, the potatoes and the creeping speedwell, lie or once lay the relics of a Roman villa. You see the treasure hunters in summer like scavenging seagulls, going over and over the surface, but they find nothing. It was dug long ago, when the plough turned up an elaborate mosaic floor. One is bound to be tempted to connect this piece of local grandeur with the dyke, but first of all we must face Crawford's argument, which cannot simply be laughed away. All the same he must be wrong, as a little excavation since his time has shown. He thought this was a fortified area of refuge, meant to defend Cirencester in the decline of Roman power against the Picts and Scots raiding the South. His boldness takes one's breath away.

And yet the rampart is not defensible, it was never defensible. It contains no fortified camp. No army existed to garrison thirty-five miles of wall. The people of Dorchester-on-Thames employed German mercenaries. That is not so far away, in fact only a night's walk that corresponds closely to one I did as a young man to see some horse races. The mounds of their defences are enormous, ours are the merest field boundaries by comparison. The area they defended is tiny compared to our twenty square miles. And one of the few things all armies have in common to this day is that they leave archaeological traces. Here there are none. Even the complete pattern of Roman farms inside and outside our ramparts is not easy to relate to

Crawford's snaking and not quite continuous line of humps and heavings in the ground. Aha, says Crawford, but this line was defending the perilous crossing of the river Evenlode at its only convenient crossing place, just above the Evenlode gorge. But I have been swimming in the Evenlode on and off now for more than thirty years. The problem is finding deep enough pools. There must be a hundred convenient crossing places and cattle splashes and stony fords.

Maybe Crawford was misled by his own method in *Wessex from the Air*. Maybe altitude and the aeroplane intoxicated him. There is no Evenlode gorge. Can he have seen it on a misty day? Could one have mistaken the dramatic and deep cuttings of the Oxford to Hereford railway for the course of the river, where the two run close together? As far as any evidence has been raked together since 1930 for the date of Grim's Dyke, it points towards the first century BC, a few minutes before the Romans arrived, or just after. Near Blenheim and near Ditchley, the rampart crosses over the poor settlements of charcoal burners or forest people of that date, not long abandoned when the long boundary wall was built. What is more, Akeman Street was cut through Grim's Dyke when Grim's Dyke already existed, and yet Akeman Street is quite an early Roman road. So if the rampart was meant for a British sanctuary, it was an ineffective one. The line is not even quite continuous.

Of course it is very hard to be sure of such a negative. Any unfinished piece of rampart might be supplied by a wooden fence, by a mesh of obstacles of any kind, even by an impenetrable thicket of briars. The evidence for the discontinuity of Grim's Dyke comes from an excavation in the 1950s at Callow Hill, about the time I was bicycling to Beaconsfield Farm. I happened to meet a lady not long ago who devoted a period of weeks to the butt end of the ditch and dyke; her part of the excavation, which was skilfully done, demonstrated there was no trace of the wall or ditch at all where they should have continued. That is the kind of job apprentice archaeologists get given. We must accept, and I am sure Crawford would now have accepted, that there were always gaps in Grim's Dyke. But we must equally accept, from the evidence of several digs in different places, that Grim's Dyke was one thing, planned by one man.

The history of speculation and conjecture on this subject is long and fascinating. Thomas Warton, who was twice Professor of Poetry at Oxford in the eighteenth century (and so was his father), wrote a parish history of Kiddington, which lies just on the far side of Ditchley, with the young Glyme running through it. He knew Grim's Dyke. His book was not a long one; it was intended for an example of what parish and county histories ought to be like. It pleases me that the corrected proofs of it, which somehow ended up in the Bodleian Library, show a message in his handwriting that must have been passed to a colleague during a college meeting some dreary winter afternoon: 'Let us clear off before Night, if possible.' Kiddington must be some ten or twelve miles from Oxford; it was Warton's parish. But the famous Stukely had been there before him, early in the century. Stukely believed that walking was the best cure for gout, and that belief had made him the greatest British archaeological authority. Thomas Warton deals with poor old Stukely rather sharply: 'Stukely believed this foss to be British, merely from his attachment to system.'

That is a more searching criticism than it looks. Warton himself thought the dyke was just a boundary, and he was the first to notice a similarity to Cranborne Chase, unexcavated territory in his time. Pitt-Rivers began to dig there only in the 1880s. That formidable warrior did cast an eye on Grim's Dyke. He thought it 'without doubt a fortification', perhaps a Roman defence against the local British. Is one wrong to observe a certain self-projection here? Was Pitt-Rivers thinking of British imperial encampments? Was Crawford also dreaming of the North-West frontier of India? And yet Pitt-Rivers might have found a closer analogy at Cranbourne Chase, which admittedly he was still to inherit. Cranbourne

Chase is one of the likeliest areas in Roman Britain for the title of imperial estate.

These estates need some explaining. Every Roman emperor inherited or assumed possession of the whole wealth of his predecessor. Their estates constantly swelled by confiscation, by punitive law, and by the right to take over all royal estates in every annexed territory, which is where Stonesfield comes in. The imperial lands in the end amounted to ten or even sixteen per cent of nearly every province in the empire. These possessions were personal, like Sandringham and Balmoral. They were administered through a special civil service parallel to the official public service. We know from inscriptions and from a written list, which set out in the fourth century the correct pecking order of Roman officials in each province, that imperial estates existed in Britain. I should have known that twenty-five years ago, because a manuscript of the same list has an illustration of Brittania which was among Denis's and my favourite postcards. Alas. To spend one's life caring more for Thomas Warton than for Roman administration is no preparation for research, even into one's own village monuments.

The emperor's estate staff were at work in Britain by the third century, but that is not early enough to explain Grim's Dyke. It leaves a leap of conjecture. Very often these estates operated as a system for controlling troublesome native areas. That seems to be what happened at Cranbourne Chase, where the garrison at Hod Hill has no other obvious function. Bokerley Dyke, which looks like a gesture of defence of that area towards the North, was not built by private enterprise. A number of scholars have carved out imperial estates of their own, here and there in Britain. The subject remains obscure. We hear of the imperial *saltus*, which means a kind of Texas range, of Wessex, and Tom Brown Stevens spoke of the imperial *saltus* of the Upper Thames Gravels. The problem remains, as he used to remark with glee, that you can dig up a Roman villa, but not its system of land tenure. It is on that maxim we need to make inroads, and once again the key to history seems to be slavery, the increase of misery. I take slavery to be the most degraded and miserable condition known to man. The Romans tortured their slaves as a matter of course. If they ran away they were crucified. When the Christian church in the late empire acquired the powers of Roman magistrates, it was employing torture within one generation. The Romans were scarcely human.

I have tried to set out the working of this long conundrum of local archaeology, and reserved what I think is the solution, in order to show on what kind of evidence it rests, and how slowly it emerges from the tangle of the countryside. At the Watt's Wells Roman villa, inside Grim's Dyke on the Ditchley estate, there were slave quarters when the place was built before 200 AD. In the fourth century the work force disappears, and so do the animals. Their sheds were pulled down and a big granary took their place. Improved agriculture? Who sowed it and who reaped it? The size of the granary indicates about five hundred and forty acres sown in a year. Under Roman farming conditions, that implies the control of about a thousand acres of arable land from one small farmhouse without slaves. Either the slaves had been moved out into barracks, a kind of concentration camp where they could be better guarded, or Watt's Wells was absorbed into some great estate. Probably both, so the slaves were in one guarded compound, centrally controlled like the working animals.

Watt's Wells villa had a front entrance that pointed directly down a path skirting through the modern village of Stonesfield. This minor road crossed the Evenlode and led directly to the Roman villa that still survives in ruins at North Leigh, a small house in the second century, with its bath in an outhouse but in the fourth century a fine big place with three wings and a courtyard. Its mosaic floors are still there to be seen. They were designed and executed in the early fourth century AD by craftsmen from Cirencester, which is another long day's walk away. Still, even at that date North Leigh was not an immense ly grand house. Nor were any of the other Roman villas inside Grim's Dyke, with the possible exception of the Stonesfield villa, which is lost.

It first surfaced on 25 January 1712, when a farmer called George Handes turned up 'an urn' with his plough. Thomas Hearne, the Oxford antiquary, visited and recorded it at once. The first coloured drawings of its mosaic floors were made under his direction and copied many times. The artist Hearne employed seems to have been called Edward Loring, but he also used Mr Burghers, the University engraver. In the same year a Mr Pointer, the chaplain of Merton College, produced a poor pamphlet with a black and white print, noting the true colours as 'Blue, red, yellow, ash, milk white, and dark brown'. 'Coins mixt with Medals of immortal Rome,' he quoted with the misplaced complacency common to chaplains of colleges, 'May clear Disputes, and teach the Times to come.' The best copy of Loring's drawing was done by George Vertue, the painter and historian of painting. His annotation is grandiloquent and moving:

'A most Exquisite Work of the Antient Romans, esteemed to be the most Elegant Piece of Antiquity of the Kind found in Great Britain. When first open'd, it was seen by Multitudes of Curious Persons, and some Learned Antiquaries have employ'd their Skill to trace out its Original Use. Now only remains this Shade, preserv'd first by the Care of Thomas Hearne MA of Oxford, and lastly by G. Vertue, Member of the Society of Antiquaries of London.'

But later in the century, the floor was uncovered again, and drawn again, by Mr W. Lewington of Woodstock, who appears to have been an architect. This time, several more rooms were recorded and the ground plan was measured. Since the complete villa has never been excavated, we can only conjecture its size and scale. On the evidence of the drawings, it was the grandest house in the district. Whoever administered or owned some huge united property inside Grim's Dyke must have lived at Stonesfield, a little east of the medieval village, not so close to the quarries. Did the slaves live where we live now? Hearne recorded that 'a great many ruins have been found all about at some furlong's distance'. One would like to know more about that, but now it is late in the day.

The trouble arose from the quarrel between George Handes and his landlord, 'one Richard Fowler of Barrington near Burford, who purchased it off one Mr Hedges, a Tailor of Oxford'. Handes renewed his lease six months before he found the pavement, but the contract had never been sealed. So knowing what lay below the soil, Handes rode over to Barrington to get a new condition added, 'that he might have leave to dig the ground'. Fowler must have thought he meant quarrying; Stonesfield and Barrington were both famous for stone at that time. 'Then the lease was sealed and Handes discovered the Treasure he had found and said he would not take five hundred pounds for it. This fired Fowler, but he could not fly off.'

So Handes charged visitors a shilling a head to see his floor, and by 1724 'some of the noble remains' had reached the Society of Antiquaries in London. Fragments must have been sold off piecemeal. The lease cannot have lasted for ever, so Handes must have gone for a quick return. Who covered the floor over, who uncovered it again, and who owned it or leased it later, I am not sure. There was another attempt to dig it in 1812, but that was abandoned. The melancholy story of the Stonesfield villa can rest at this point. All we have is the drawings, some awkward and some fine, of a floor on which the native British would not have been allowed to walk. The craze for Roman antiquities in eighteenth-century England was part of a web of romantic passions which included the passion for solitude. There was a tendency at that time for the rich and grand to live alone with their servants out of sight. Beckford had his lawns mown at night, to keep his gardens solitary. And which was the duke who sacked all servants automatically, if ever he met one around the house? Like an unconscious ballet of the fourth century AD.

The origins of Grim's Dyke, which stirred up all this roundabout research, and more of it which I will spare the reader, must have been simpler. Inside the East-end Gate of Blenheim, that is the gate near the east end of the village of Combe, grow some of the finest and most ancient oak trees in England. For about a mile they tangle their arthritic branches in whatever a very old tree can feel of air or sun. These living monuments are very much earlier than the title of Duke of Marlborough. They are all that is left of an ancient hunting forest of the kings of England. In the Domesday Book, Woodstock, Cornbury, and Wichwood are all king's forests. In the Middle Ages, the forest of Wichwood, that is the area where the very harsh forest laws of the Normans were in force, extended far beyond Cornbury and Woodstock, as far as Great Tew, but that huge region was a Norman invention. Before the Normans, Woodstock belonged to the Anglo-Saxon kings. King Aethelred held a council at Woodstock fifty years before 1066. There is no time between 100 BC and 1000 AD when such a forest would have been planted by man or established by nature. We can be reasonably sure that the ancestors of these great oaks stood where they now stand before the Romans plunged into the surf.

Was Grim's Dyke a tribal territory, a little kingdom marked out by newcomers? There is some evidence for a Germanic tribe who fought their way inland in this direction, in the fifty years before the Romans came. But the water rights that Grim's Dyke encloses imply familiar knowledge of a wide area. In fact only the water-sources they enclosed give logic to the thirty-five miles of rampart. At Cornbury, at Ramsden, at the Roman building above Shakenoak Farm, and at Field Farm, Grim's Dyke lays claim to water. Was the rampart to keep animals in or out? Was this always a hunting forest? Or a great range for farming? The few pre-Roman remains suggest the tribal lands of a people who were not rich, but the rampart suggests an overlord who was powerful. I assume that the ditch and the rampart were dug by slave labour.

And what happened to that people? In the course of centuries, the Roman presence in these parts became dense. Silver coins have been found under Woodstock church commemorating the capture of Jerusalem. The Romans are said to have left the Evenlode valley their edible snails. I have sometimes seen those in the fields, though not for many years now; maybe they went native like the rest of us. The Romans probably took over Grim's Dyke as a boundary of some sort. It is perfectly possible that it was or became an imperial estate. If the Romans disliked the rampart, they would have demolished it. As for the Germanic tribe, one must assume they bled somewhere. Or did they vanish like deer into the forest shadows? Shakespeare says that deer can weep.

CHAPTER NINE

The Shadow of the Sea

I HAVE FALLEN too much into the mood of Thomas Warton. He had no claim to greatness. As a poet, he was a quiet disciple of Thomas Gray, and lowing herds wind slowly through his poems. As a scholar, he traced English poetry back beyond Pope, through Milton and Spenser and Chaucer into the still unknowable Middle Ages. His tiny parish church at Kiddington has some ancient and unlikely animal heads nestling under its eaves that recall Kilpeck. He wrote odes for royal birthdays, one on George III sea-bathing at Yarmouth, one on solitude, one on a romantic suicide halfway between Gray's peasant and the scholar gipsy. He seems to have loved country people, and this particular countryside. In *The Hamlet, written in Whichwood Forest*, he wrote:

> When morning's twilight-tinctured beam
> Strikes their low thatch with slanting gleam,
> They rove abroad in ether blue,
> To dip the scythe in fragrant dew;
> The sheaf to bind, the beech to fell,
> That nodding shades a craggy dell.

It was the kind of verse several eighteenth-century parsons could write, and none the worse for that. There are no women in the poem, but it has a purity and exactness which are unusual. 'They spy the squirrel's airy bounds.' Maybe Warton never grew up; his virtues are boyish. He was famous for beer and pipes and sitting in pothouses; he preferred the company of Thames watermen to that of college fellows. But he also wrote an ode on Fountains Abbey, a sonnet on Dugdale's Monasticon, and another on Stonehenge. I wish I had known that twenty-seven years ago, when I first liked Warton because of an absurd but somehow moving Latin poem of his about the river Cherwell. There has been no room for the Cherwell in this book, but the Cherwell, the Evenlode and the Windrush valleys define what I think of as home ground. It is good to see that Warton, who can make little sense of Stonehenge – 'Studious to trace thy wondrous origin, We muse on many an ancient tale renown'd,' – does at least think it the noblest monument in Britain. He sees it as an ancient Westminster Abbey, not so much a memorial, or a place of sacrifice or burial, as a place of crowning. Yet one cannot help liking and welcoming Thomas Warton, if only because life and literature, naïve relish and polished expression so intermingle in his verses, and for him all British antiquities belonged to the countryside in which they were set.

> Nor rough, nor barren, are the winding ways
> Of hoar Antiquity, but strewn with flowers.

In five years of constant journeys in pursuit of ancient places in this country I have certainly found that to be true. For a year or so I was *The Times* archaeological correspondent. It was not much of a job, because one was payed only for what they printed, and archaeology had a very low priority. It used to appear only on the Court Page, which was run by an ancient old man in a black coat with dandruffed shoulders, who I suspect wrote most of the page himself. The only time I ever called at his office, he seemed extremely surprised to see anyone. My work was mostly to make a readable digest of obscurely published reports I thought promising, and sometimes to extract information from excavating archaeologists, many of whom I found prickly. The most interesting thing I learnt, from the nicest young archaeologist I encountered at that time, was that the jam-labels Pitt-Rivers used to stick on bits of pottery were so strongly glued they had to be removed by sand-blasting before the pottery could be chemically tested. How pleased Pitt-Rivers would have been at a systematic dating system for nineteenth-century excavations according to the power of the glue.

By now I have travelled nearly all over England, most of Wales and much of Scotland. The most amazing landscape discovery of my middle age has been Derbyshire, the intricate patchwork of stone walls high up in the lower Peak District, the Mercian or should one say Viking stonework in the churches, and the sun falling and quenching itself somewhere behind the next valley. One can almost hear the sun hiss. That is the true heart of England I suppose, and the cradle of Robin Hood. It is resistance country. I see why the Scots under Charles Edward Stuart refused to move south of Derby. They were unhappy out of sight of the southern tip of the Pennines, the last proper rocks in England as you come south. The river Dove is the border of Derbyshire and Staffordshire. Near Ilam, at the opening of Dovedale, you can see two completely different kinds of landscape from one spot, the rocky barrier of Pennine hilltops to the north, and a gentler surge of green swellings to the south, where the hills begin to carry groves of trees. In 1917, the entire Staffordshire Regiment was wiped out, nearly to a man, between dawn and dusk of one day.

The most impressive single monument I have seen in Britain in nearly thirty years is Maiden Castle. The height of its turf battlements and the frightening depths of its ditches are unforgettable. It feels as if it were balanced in blue ether, whatever Warton meant by that. Perhaps he meant Leafield, which was a hamlet in his time and the highest point in Oxfordshire. The sadness of Maiden Castle is its fall to the Romans. The ritual use of Hambledon Hill is another matter. That must have been a terrible sight, an earthly thundercloud, a place abandoned to the dead. Why was it built like a hillfort? Was it a memorial of war, an empty Troy decorated with dead men's heads? Today those terrific grass slopes look like a pastoral fantasy, like the steep grass at Maiden Castle. The true reason why I was delighted to write about archaeology for *The Times* is that Thomas Hardy wrote them a report once on the dig at Maiden Castle, which deserves a high place among his prose writings. In that piece he conveys a sense of the landscape and of human suffering in the landscape even more strongly than in his novels. One can feel the texture of earth and flint.

And yet of all my archaeological journeys the most insistent memory is of flints the sea washes, and the rumble and retiring roar of the North Sea on pebble banks at Aldeburgh. Under those pebbles lies the old town. East Anglia is cut off from most of England by the suburban sprawl that creeps northward from London; I had never been as far as the coast until two or three years ago. East Suffolk is a mysterious and rather impenetrable countryside, impregnated with melancholy and loneliness, and with great beauty unlike any other. I stayed at Aldeburgh in a golfing hotel near the end of the town, where the mist wreathed in the evening and the road gave out, in the setting of an M. R. James ghost story. Every morning we woke to the crying of gulls round the fishermen's huts on the pebbles, mile beyond mile of tan brown, black, and grey and white stones. Inland, there were crumbling Saxon churches, isolated by stretches of water, white plumes, yellow reeds. It was through these waters that the Viking ships had made their way in, spied on from the watch towers of the churches. The ship burials seems to have been always at the furthest point inland such a great swan-necked ship could creep from the North Sea. The sea at Aldeburgh has a cold glitter more ominous than the Atlantic wildness, it has a deadly look.

It was not only Sutton Hoo and Orford and the burial mounds that brought me into East Anglia. It was also the pattern of the country as it alters a little way inland, and the special architecture. I wish Wolsey had lived to build his great college at Ipswich, and I could even wish he had used East Anglian builders for the chapel he intended on the north side of his quadrangle at Christ Church. But he came late in the day. Renaissance angels were already sulking on the wall of Christ

Church when the Cardinal lost power. The only piece of Suffolk architecture near Oxford is the church at Ewelme which the Duke of Suffolk built in the fifteenth century. In the great churches of East Anglia, at Grundisburgh and at Blythburgh, the angels hover in the roof like glittering Christmas stars. Suffolk churches glitter with a light now inside and out, but in 1500 all the plain glass was coloured; the outer walls were sober though they were handsome, and the inner walls were covered over with bold and lucid decoration.

So I do not really think Lord Clark can be right when he says of them, 'horizontal buildings, like rigid cages of light', that they were no longer being built to house mysteries, but for preaching and the new intellectual devotion, as if they awaited the coming reform. Holland certainly feels closer to the Suffolk coast in most ways than London, and European voices confuse the English radio there. But the old mysteries were once at home in those churches. Now with their plain glass and the low land around them they are almost more impressive. At Grundisburgh at dusk the angels seem to hover like bats among the beams. Blythburgh church is like a great flinty sea bird on its untidy nest above the water meadows. When the sun shines after rain, its wet and flashing stones have a finer texture than any other building I know except maybe for Strata Florida, which is Welsh monastic ruins. From outside the church at Blythburgh, one can see clear through both sets of upper windows to the sky beyond. When the Reformation came, strangers arrived at this village, and the great wooden angels in the roof were shot down like wild birds. Their broken wings were found in the eighteenth century, peppered with lead shot. The original colours are still visible, like faded moth colours. Is our history not as terrible as any nation's? And yet there is an innocence about it.

It is worth wondering how such things happen, what kind of rage it is that makes people shoot down painted wooden angels out of their dark blue sky. It seems a gesture of defiance, but against what? Town against country, progress against conservative peasantry? Peasant rage against the sufferings of their lives? In the Domesday Book, which name incidentally already suggests black humour on the part of the English, Suffolk had the most churches of any county in England, that is four hundred. Suffolk also had the most people, sixty thousand at the rate of a hundred and fifty to a church. They can hardly have all been heath or forest dwellers, but Suffolk is rich in nooks and corners. The monastery at Iken existed in the seventh century, and controlled houses as far away as Much Wenlock in the Welsh Marches. One would not think so to look at Iken today. In the English Civil War this countryside was strong against the monarchy. Reform was absolute in East Anglia. What had happened? I am not able to solve this historical problem, though I can think of solutions, all of them unhappy, and many tricks of unhappy evidence.

One of the most pleasure-giving and at the same time one of the obscurest of the British antiquities I know is Whitsbury Rings on the edge of Hampshire. The country round about is varied and curiously secretive. Long strings of racehorses move out onto the sullen downs. A wood of wild yew trees casts forty foot shadows on the gorse and turf. Old houses and Roman farms lie hidden in the deep lanes. We drove there one night during a wild storm when every oak tree was threshing and every lane was littered with green branches. I first saw Whitsbury Rings in early summer, when the woods and the ditch under the ramparts were full of bluebells and the pale trunks of beech and ash were gleaming in the first proper sunshine of the year. The centre of what must once have been a formidably large enclosure belongs to a stud farm. Thoroughbred horses sniffed and snuffed at our tiny dog. The stud at Whitsbury paid £780,000 for a horse the other day. Whitsbury Rings may be the only ancient hillfort in England still being used for its ancient purpose, the breeding of horses.

Some of the most impressive antiquities we have in the English countryside are the ruins of long, ramparted avenues, with monumental stones at the end. We know by excavation that these places were built by a pastoral, not an agricultural people, long before the Druids. Their relation to astronomy and mathematics is a buried metaphor, a symbol, maybe a belief. It is like saying as Pliny does that oysters swell and diminish with the increase and diminution of the moon and the lunar pull of the tides. Is he thinking of the lunar lustre of mother-of-pearl, or a pearl itself like a perfect full moon, or just of the strange sexual life of oysters? But what he says is true; it is the observation of nature. There is a sense in which sympathetic magic follows natural laws. I take those long avenues to play a vital part in the farming of horses and cattle that roamed about freely for most of the year. They are devices to show ownership and perhaps to control breeding. All ritual, all religion, all monuments, had to do with that, even Stonehenge itself. The mind of man could not reach further in those simple days. Terrible things were done, but the core of life was innocent, its heat was natural. Now there is nothing left of those people but the blackish-green yew trees against the olive grass of the downs in a dry summer. Later ages have withered them away.

Art is a solution after all. What is hard and sad to express in words can be expressed in painting. The most primitive landscapes in England are terribly shrunken. Eggardon Hill carries a camp which is a minor version of Maiden Castle. It rises up north of the road between Bridport and Dorchester, nearly due north of Litton Cheney, which was a place of pilgrimage to us when my wife's friend Reynolds Stone lived there. Everything around him seemed to express him. He was famous as a printer and engraver; as a friend he had an immediate generosity of intelligence. The Victorian embossed bindings, the toast and honey, and the inherited ancient pottery of his house would have made a strong enough impression, but his garden, part of which was nearly completely wild, made a stronger one. He was famous for the austerest of woodcuts, but in his life he took to painting at Litton Cheney, and the wild garden lives and he lives in those paintings. The page headings of *The*

Times used to look everlasting, and the woodcuts expressed the man as only a severe discipline can do, but in those wilderness paintings he set himself free, I imagine. He was one of those 'whose individual voice tells me I too am individual'.

The land under Eggardon Hill is wilder still. It is called Powerstock Forest. It is all strange shapes of oak and livid or dark mossy boughs, sedges, fallow deer, hawks, and buzzards. Powerstock Forest is like a jungle, though only ninety acres are left of it, and those only because Kenneth Allsop protested so strongly about them. In such a place, one would sooner be a painter than an archaeologist. The rest of the old landscape has been cleared and drained by the National Forestry for coniferous woods. The conifers are a curious bit of policy, and economically not very sound. The only customer for those trees is the paper industry. But suppose trees were cheaper elsewhere? Suppose there were fewer papers, or another way of making paper?

Far-reaching changes do affect our landscapes, as anyone can see who observes the scab of modern houses around every North-Oxfordshire village. The older council houses are the best and the least pretentious. But there were always changes. In Italy, the compact two-storey house divided into rooms like a Stonesfield village house drove out the old long houses only in the fifteenth century. In Ireland and Wales you can still find genuine long houses with the cattle in one end and the people in the other. Our maid Mary Morrissey went to a wake in her Irish village in the forties where a hen flew out from under the dead man's bed. In France, the long houses went in the early sixteenth century, in England not before 1575. Small wonder Shakespeare lived in New House. All the same, his England was splendidly provincial. The Globe Theatre was roofed with thatch and whitewashed like a cattle shed. And when the big change did come and the suburbs began to swell, then infant mortality rose like a line on a fever chart. Cholera in Oxford was a nineteenth-century problem. The long exodus out of slavery and exploitation has ended only in our own lifetimes, and it has left us bewildered.

Long pondering over the bones of all the British islands and provinces, and long archaeological journeys, the reading of innumerable books, bring one back always to the successive waves of destruction, to the flutes of autumn. The poet Trakl killed himself because he was unable to bear the First World War. He was an Austrian, and after Grodek, one of the first great battles of 1914, he was left alone as a medical orderly, in charge of a barn full of badly wounded men, whose pain he was unable to relieve. The poem he wrote about Grodek is an elegy for many European battles, above all for the unborn, the might-have-beens which every battle ended, the generations of the unborn. *And in the reeds the dark flutes of autumn mutter their undertone.* What makes us tragic and pathetic is the reality of our hope. Trakl died by suicide, but I think he is the poet of innocence, he is William Blake in 1914.

In the last summer these themes were on my mind during a journey to Scotland, where I went with our small family to work on a new edition of Boswell and Johnson in the Western Islands. Many old lessons were rammed home yet again. It was a dark, rain-smitten journey, by Crickley Hill, where the gateposts of the Iron Age fort were carved out of huge entire oak trees, past the secretive ancient churches of the Severn Valley, with stone sculpture like spume from the Bristol Channel. When the wind blows strongly from the west, you can taste the Bristol Channel on your lips on the hills around Oxford. We passed places in Lancashire I had forgotten for twenty years.

The wildness of old Lancashire had its advantages, in hospitality of an almost feudal kind, and in mutual love and loyalty such as I do not believe I have ever seen anywhere else. The poet Spenser, who typically of his age was an unsuccessful English colonist in Ireland, had his early patronage from the Nowell family of Pendleton, which is not far from Stonyhurst, in his time a forest castle, as I have said. There exists a plausible argument, which I am slightly inclined to credit, that the young Shakespeare could have spent some of his so-called lost years in the service of the Houghton family of Lee Hall, Preston, not at all distant from Pendleton. The family there kept a troop of players for a time. It was an extravagant but not a fantastical whim to keep players. What else would it mean to tell oneself one was civilized in Lancashire in the sixteenth century? Why else did the Esterhazy family retain Mozart? One finds the Macleods of Dunvegan behaving in much the same way in the early eighteenth century. But the patronage of these unreformed old houses does say something about England, and how primitive it was so late in the day. Shakespeare had heard blind harpers. The Renaissance, so far as it filtered through to London, was the more shock to him.

We rested a few days on our way north in the Lake District, not far from Grasmere. No writer can help being interested in Wordsworth and his cottage, because of the small physical and the ambitious spiritual scale of his life. I must own to having been put off this poet recently by a volume of dull letters, by his alliance with the Arnold family, and by his own tendency to beget bishops and headmasters. But I have never doubted his greatness, though I never much relished it. In the Lakes, where he was born, he comes into his own. Sometimes I wish he had lived to know Beatrix Potter as a neighbour, though I prefer her prose to his, and dread to think what poetic versions he might have made of her stories. She seems truer than he does to the English countryside as I have known it; but the wildness of his times is hardly imaginable now, except in bad weather in passes between those long dramatic lakes.

For years I used to think that the Lakes, which incidentally are far more open to the north than they are southwards, were a British sanctuary that not even the Romans had penetrated. Maybe the idea arose from *Wordsworth's Guide to the Lakes*; he seems to have taken it from the 1788 guide by West, which he quotes for its 'centuries of solitude' broken only by the mutual slaughter of wild animals and birds. The Celtic tribes, says Wordsworth, 'became joint tenants with the wolf, the boar, the wild bull, the red deer, and the leigh, a gigantic species of deer which has long been extinct'. The Romans, he feels, encouraged the British to improve their manners and their agriculture, but hardly ventured into the inner lakes 'except for military purposes, or in subservience to the profiit they drew from the mines'. The truth is that their roads, some of them wild ones, can be traced across the passes, and Roman civilian buildings as well as the camp that Wordsworth knew have recently been found at Ambleside. The track by Skelwith Bridge and Wrynose Bottom leads from Ambleside to the sea. Castle Howe guards it, and Castle Howe is Roman. Still, most of the place names are British: Derwent from an oak tree, Cocker from crooked, Grasmere half British and half Scandinavian, Keswick a Scandinavian spelling of cesewic, British for a cheese farm. One gets a sense of sanctuary. In the good old days, the old people said to Wordsworth, a squirrel could have travelled from Wytheburn chapel to Keswick without ever touching the ground.

Alas there was nowhere in England left unpenetrated by the Romans or unravaged afterwards. Beyond the Lakes to the east rises Stainmore purple and forbidding; that is still formidably wild country, it contains natural solitudes. At Brough under Stainmore a twelfth-century castle restored in the seventeenth still stands in the ruins of the Roman fort of Verterae. At Bowes a twelfth-century keep rises from another Roman castle. These places are like Pevensey and Porchester, the old Roman forts of the Saxon shore. Their tragic story is continuous. And between the Romans and the iron rule of the Normans this was the kingdom of Northumbria, which the Vikings ruined. Or perhaps it was half Norse already. It was not Christianity in Britain, to judge from the bloodcurdling poetry of the day, but settled farming that was the great civilizing influence of the Dark Ages, a most lamentably slow influence. One could learn something from the squirrels in the oak trees, the deer in the forest, the slaves.

Stocking to stocking, jersey to jersey,
head to a hard arm,
they kiss under the rain,
bruised by their marble bed.
In Garsdale, dawn;
at Hawes, tea from the can.
Rain stops, sacks
steam in the sun, they sit up.
Copper-wire moustache,
sea-reflecting eyes
and Baltic plainsong speech
declare: by such rocks
men killed Bloodaxe . . .

In Basil Bunting's poem the death of Bloodaxe has great dignity. He was 'King of York, King of Dublin, King of Orkney'. Nothing could put so clearly the strangely fragmented Britain of the tenth century, at the height of the Scandinavian invasions. Eric Bloodaxe was a Norwegian King deposed and exiled for his bloody violence, who gathered himself an army of the murderous and the dispossessed. He took and held Northumbria for a time and reigned two years at York in defiance of the Vikings of Dublin as well as the English. The appalling disturbance of these Viking kingdoms had two far-reaching consequences. They made it inevitable that whatever terrifying monarch unified England would also pursue Viking power as far as Dublin and as far as Scotland: the problems of Ireland have a continuous history from that time. The remnant of the Viking kingdoms lying in the English soil, and whatever there is of Viking blood and custom in the English people, are probably, because those tribes were so ungovernable, the beginning of our democracy.

In extreme regions like the Orkneys, 'the sea bled, streamed dark on the planknails, sobbed with blood on the bulwark-shields of the boats'. They lived out their gruesome saga for many generations. Eric Bloodaxe lost Northumbria after two years, no one is sure how. Two hundred years later he was said to have been killed by Maccus son of Olaf, an earl who was perhaps the son of the equally villainous King of Dublin. He was killed by treachery in a waste place called Steinmor. By such rocks men killed Bloodaxe. His death, at which the saints doubtless rejoiced in their graves though Homer might have lamented him, was the end of an age. His was the last lifetime in which any adventurer, with a following of landless or ambitious men, might become the father of a dynasty in England. 'Flame ravaged, smoke reared reaking skyward, wolves dined on the dead.' But a little less wildly, a little less often, after the death of Bloodaxe.

Maybe all our journeys are towards a lost paradise, where an angel with a sword will mark our arrival. Mine was towards innocent places, to the west coast of Scotland, to the most peaceful of lake islands, north of Ledaig and looking towards Lismore. Beyond the loch the mountains brood like vast grazing animals. Otters play in the water at times and you can hear the seals barking from the next island. Lismore carried an early monastery. Indeed the mere sight of such an island might seduce anyone to sit on a rock and read psalms and eat seaweed for the rest of his life. Its secret is limestone. The monks on Lismore came from Iona, which is hardly a day's sail away, beyond the misty shapes of the hills on Mull. One can imagine that they stole inland into perfect quiet; was it to be out of the way of sea-raiders or out of sight of Ireland? Or was it on a missionary quest? Were the bells heard clanging from far up the loch? The medieval Welsh kept the handbells of the early monks as their holiest relics. I imagine those intemperate Irish faces, furious with heaven-hunger, as they clanged and clanged. But another reason may exist why the monks chose out Lismore. They will have known a series of ancient monuments on the mainland that suggest a track or roadway of the dead, with the mounds of prehistoric tombs beside it. They knew another on the mainland opposite Iona, coming down by Loch Nell, the loch of swans, to the seashore. Many chiefs and kings of Scotland and lords of the isles were buried on Iona as long as the monks lasted and later. Were these places holy islands before the monks ever settled on them? I am inclined to think so.

The old standing stones all over Scotland are mostly the relics of graves. It is not surprising there are more of them than even Crawford's Dark Age map and the Ordnance Survey map record. Later in time, we can see the same rough standing stones carved with Viking runes and serpents, with the lettering called Ogham, and sometimes in Wales with Latin as well. Pagans reused Christian stones with powerful effect, and Christians used pagan images. The stones remained the same; meaning cannot exhaust a stone. But a road to an island, with grave mounds and stone markers beside it, makes little sense of the island as a burial place. Why were some of the dead, and apparently among the noblest of the dead, buried by the roadside with great monuments when the sea was already in sight? One would think that the road was a sort of pilgrimage of the dead, that it hardly mattered whether one arrived. It appears that the islands were a beginning of the other world, well placed perhaps for setting out on that journey. The clansmen took their chief so far along his way and buried him where he could wait by the quayside. Suppose that the souls of the dead streamed away into the sunset like migrating birds, uttering the cries of birds. The dark and cold country where the sun sinks into the sea was a place of freshness. No other refuge existed.

We do in fact know something about these islands in very ancient times. The historian Plutarch was a priest at Delphi, and in the year 84 AD he recorded a conversation there about the death of gods and the silence of oracles. One of those who took part was Demetrios of Tarsus, who had been to Britain under Agricola. He dedicated two small bronze tablets covered with silver to the gods at York, which happen to have survived: one to 'the Gods of the Governor's court' and the other to 'Ocean and the Sea-goddess'. What he told Plutarch was that the islands off Britain were uninhabited and scattered in the sea. He had visited 'the island nearest to the uninhabited ones', which sounds like Mull or Skye, on an official mission. Its few inhabitants were holy men, exempt from British sea-raiding. They told him that a great storm with 'signs in heaven, violent winds and waterspouts', which he witnessed, must mark the death of one of their gods.

I had read all this years ago and forgotten it. I was therefore much surprised to observe the other day the next thing that Demetrios was told: 'That there was one island there, where Kronos lies prisoner, guarded by a hundred-handed monster, and asleep; for sleep has been devised as a chain to bind him; and around him lie many lesser gods as his attendants and his servants.' Kronos is the same father of Zeus whose sleepy hill broods over Olympia, the god of the golden age, whose tower is the Hill of Kronos. Here he seems to be the Earthfather from whom the Gauls claimed to be descended. There are similar stories about holy men, who 'dress in long black tunics and walk with a staff, looking like the Furies in a tragedy', and another mysterious empty island, recorded a little earlier about the Tin Islands, which seem to be the Scilly Isles. Later in time, but still under the Romans, there was said to be a specially holy race of men on Lundy Island, who refused trade and had visions of the future. To the Greeks and Romans, holiness meant the refusal to trade for money. Immunity from war was mysterious to them; innocence was mysterious.

The variety and beauty of the world we have inherited is after all puzzling to consider. The intense, wandering light that falls from between clouds on the highlands of Scotland is enough in itself to make one think. There are few forest animals left alive. I have once seen a wildcat, but never a pine marten. Many new animals have established themselves in Britain in this century. There are Japanese deer loose in the Midlands, and beavers, mink, and God knows what else in the rivers. Our hares still squat sagaciously in the cold fields before it snows, and the rabbits are back in the hedges. By Roman law no one could own a wild animal. It was there for the taking;

you were free to kill it or to take it. Badger-baiting died out in this countryside only in my lifetime. And yet a wood near Stonesfield nurses a mysterious family of snow-white pheasants. The races of men in these islands are at least as unexpected as the animal species. Britannia has her toes in the surf of the cold sea, and whatever the sea carries comes to her. Her past is terrifying, it is almost too bad to be meditated, but the grass has grown over most of it.

APPENDIX

Requiem Sermon for David Jones

Erit autem agnus absque
macula, masculus anniculus

Exodus xii. 5

David Jones understood better than the rest of us the sacrifice of the lamb. His experience in the 1914 war was terrible and it was deep. He understood and he needed what is offered at the stone of this altar and what is shared at the table of this altar and what is said and what is sung in the petrified forest of this church. His need was quite innocent, merely human, to do what has already been done once and for all on another hilltop, outside a different city, and also done many times from the beginning of mankind. In its reality and in its meaning that long series of sacrifices has not ended. *Erit autem agnus absque macula, masculus anniculus*. The man who does not know this has not understood anything.

We are doing here what is done elsewhere and what has been done. When the priest comes to the holy words of Christ's institution, to the consecration of the sacrament, his will is and his meaning is simply to do what the Church does, there is nothing personal in what he intends, any more than in what he accomplishes. He means what is meant by the assembly of the saints of God in this church. He does in another form what the painters in the caves of Lascaux already did for their fellows, only now substantially:

> And see how they run, the juxtaposed forms brighting the vaults of Lascaux; how the linear is wedded to volume, how they do, within, in an unbloody manner, under the forms of brown haematite and black manganese on the graved lime-face, what is done without,
>
> far on the windy tundra
>
> at the kill
>
> that the kindred may have life.

Is it very remote to illuminate the early emergence of man on this planet from what we understand of the Mass? And when the Mass, which really we understand so little, and which alone transforms the universe, has thrown its light into those pure and dark beginnings, how intense or how faint a light does our understanding of man in his beginnings reflect onto this congregation's knowledge of itself? Yet human nature must make some sense; how else can the universe be understood? What is performed here has for its meaning and scope the metamorphosis of mankind. It is the beginning of the marriage supper of the lamb who was sacrificed. *Erit autem agnus absque macula, masculus anniculus.*

David is sleeping soundly with the first dead. He was astonishingly innocent. In his paintings there was a vigorous innocence, and in his poetry always the same purity of eye. As a painter and a writer there was something completely genuine about him. His great learning and his wisdom, and those rambling discursive intuitions that he felt so strongly about had a childlike quality. That extraordinary personal sweetness of his had something very fresh about it. In his poem *Rite and Fore-time* he prayed for the prehistoric dead. Today we shall pray for him and them together:

From before time
his perpetual light
shines upon them.
Upon all at once
upon each one
whom he invites, bids, us to recall
when we make the recalling of him
daily, at the Stone.
When the offerant
our *servos*, so theirs whose life is changed not taken away
is directed to say
Memento etiam.
After which it is allowed him then to say *Nobis quoque.*

David Jones worked at more branches of art than any comparable artist in Britain since William Blake. In certain ways he was very like Blake. He had the same density of thoughts and inventions and always the same streak of rude rationality, the same interest in craft and technique, and if any artist has been in this century, he was a visionary writer as he was a visionary painter. All that is important to us, more than today it is to him. Indeed, since I believe that greatness in any art is to be defined in terms of particular hungers and needs of the great mass of mankind in a given generation being satisfied by a particular artist, then I am inclined to believe that David Jones was a very great artist. But David was a unique human being, and what he accomplished in his art was a direct projection of what he was as a man. What is that quality? His sensibility was as cold and vigorous as the early morning and his intuition was deep and immediate because it was simple, because it was genuine.

This wonderful church is not so great or so simple or so deep or so cold a monument as Stonehenge. We are the prisoners of every part of our history. History is not absolved, it is a one-way process. How did we come to these terrible deserts of brick and marble from that grass and those great rocks? David Jones understood that, and he saw in what way one was present in the other. He believed and we may say that he knew the points at which this world in its reality and history is most intelligible and most penetrable, the point where it runs backward into its origins, the point at which the whole world suffers its metamorphosis not into fire, not into ice, but otherwise, in an unbloody manner at this stone, at this church, on this black battlefield.

In 1914 the whole youth of Europe, the simple children of simple people were led out into a muddy place and commanded to slaughter one another; to that enormous crisis David Jones was an innocent witness. When we pray for him we must pray also for that generation and for ourselves. On the day Christ was crucified the soldiers in his execution squad had once been children in remote villages.

We must pray also for that generation and for ourselves. Today the greenness of the world is running dry. We have accepted to be lost. David Jones had these words written above his bed: *Hora novissima, tempora pessima sunt: vigilemus*. When we pray for David today, for everlasting light, freshness and peace, we must pray also for ourselves: that we should have courage, and take on some likeness to the sacrifice we offer: *agnus absque macula, masculus anniculus*.

My dear brethren, human religion is not the same as poetry, perhaps it may be older, it is not an art. Poetry is only language and religion is more than a language. It has a more substantial reality. The process of this world is real, and Christ will come to judge the world by fire and by his justice. Our trust and the water that will sprinkle us in that fire is the mercy of God, and the blood that Christ has let drop for us. Our trust is in the mercy and judgement of Christ. The vision of his compassion belongs to innocent eyes and it belongs also to us because our innocence can be renewed. The man who does not know this has not understood anything.

David Jones had a devoted, suffering life. He was full of gaiety and sweetness throughout many years of physical and mental illness. He was the friendliest and most loving of human beings and he was terribly lonely. Many of the things he most cared about crashed into ruins in his lifetime. He was too deep and too truthful an artist not to despair and yet he was possessed continually by the drifting light of an unexplained hope. He had that unusual and simple and admirable courage that seems to belong to epic poems. He worked like a hermit in a cave, but a very sociable hermit. He rejoiced in tiny luxuries, he loved his friends, he turned his face to the light. He was so patient that his face became saint-like and David smiling transfigures every memory of him. Now he is with God; that is the most serious thing you can say about any human being. We must pray for him and we must pray for ourselves.

It is not the tradition of the Church that a sermon at the Mass for any dead man should be a panegyric. We are here to recall in the sight of God only a friend, a brother, one of ourselves. But if we never learn to see Christ in one another we shall never see his face. Seeing him, learning to believe in him, we ask for mercy, and it is Christ who asks for mercy. In one man's life, a whole human tradition can live or die out or come to a late, intense flowering, so that the rest of the world knows it in that man's life in whom it was dying. Christ is in those traditions, asking as a child asks for the mercy of God, calling down that blessing. David Jones's tradition was Welsh. He is a last innocent witness to the cultural massacre of the Welsh people by the English and by the modern world. But in David's life the whole Welsh thing became something different, more intense, more suffering and more noble than we had known it to be. That is the work of Christ, it is the Spirit of God crying out to the Father.

And if there is nothing left in all this but Christ, shall we be so very lonely? There is more reality in David Jones's poems and his thoughts, and a fresher reality in his paintings, than our powers of perception can deal with. In his technical understanding of the